PRAISE FOR *WE WANT TO DO MORE THAN SURVIVE*

"Through unflinching and daring inquiry, Dr. Bettina Love has stepped out on faith to articulate our pain, suffering, and eternal search for joy. Her words resurrect the abolitionist credo of 'education' over 'school.' Because they are two different things, the question remains: can school be the place where education happens or do we need to radically rethink what we're doing? Dr. Love's work suggests that if we do not choose the latter, we are complicit in our own demise."

> —**DAVID STOVALL**, professor of African American studies and criminology, law, and justice, University of Illinois at Chicago, and coauthor of *Twenty-First-Century Jim Crow Schools*

"This book is exactly what we need: a powerful indictment of our education system as an industry that robs dark children of their potential. Dr. Love challenges us to become abolitionists by holding ourselves and our colleagues accountable for our complicity in perpetuating the 'educational survival complex.' As educators, we must recognize the impact of whiteness on our classrooms, demand the impossible, welcome the struggle, and refuse to oppress dark children by calling out racism, recognizing our students' cultures and histories, and showing them they matter to our communities and to our world. This isn't about reform; it's about freedom, and I'm moving from ally to coconspirator. Every educator needs to read this book, to freedom dream, and to challenge oppression with intersectional justice."

> —**MANDY MANNING**, 2018 National Teacher of the Year

"This much-needed book is at once personal, analytic, poetic, exacting, and soaring. Dr. Bettina Love brilliantly weaves, in artisanal and scholarly fashion, the threads and fabric of history, the present, and the possible future. She weaves in a way that we are invited to understand what moving past survival means, in personal, communal, and nation-building ways. Th⋯ ⋯ a call to building a different future: one made for free⋯

> —**LEIGH PATEL**, autho⋯

"This book is a treasure! With rigorous⋯ criticism, and brave personal reflection⋯ dares us to dream and struggle toward⋯ ⋯educa-tional freedom. With the mind of a scho⋯ ⋯a revolutionary, Bettina Love has penned a book that pl⋯ ⋯her in the tradition of Freire, Giroux, hooks, and Ladson-Billings. This beautiful text also affirms her position as one of the leading education scholars of her generation."

> —**MARC LAMONT HILL**, author of *Nobody: Casualties of America's War on the Vulnerable, from Ferguson to Flint and Beyond*

"*We Want To Do More Than Survive* is endarkened feminist wisdom in dark times. In the tradition of a skilled kente weaver, Dr. Love brings together abolitionist traditions of educational freedom work with contemporary struggles for Black humanity and creates a stunning tribute to the absolute necessity of joy and love in resistance struggles. What sets this book apart is Love's critical understanding that the splendor of kente is seen not in the weaver's individual efforts or strips of cloth, but instead when those pieces are woven together to illuminate our larger narrative as people of color in community. That narrative of Black freedom dreaming is this book you hold in your hands. And it is a must-read for those who love dark people, who love education, and who love the possibilities of educational freedom as intersectional justice right now."

—**CYNTHIA B. DILLARD** (Nana Mansa II of Mpeasem, Ghana),
Mary Frances Early Endowed Professor of Teacher Education,
University of Georgia, and author of *On Spiritual Strivings:
Transforming an African American Woman's Academic Life*

"A useful rejoinder, half a century on, to Paulo Freire's *Pedagogy of the Oppressed*; deserving of a broad audience among teachers and educational policymakers."

—*KIRKUS REVIEWS*

"Bettina Love has managed to write a book that is both a love song to our children and a potent weapon. Part memoir, part manual, part manifesto, *We Want to Do More Than Survive* explains that abolitionist teaching is neither a new set of standards nor a social justice curriculum, but a revolutionary commitment to transforming ourselves, our country, and the world. Written in breathtaking prose and bold cadences, it reminds us that 'mattering' is a verb, and making sure all of our kids truly matter is unfinished business for which we are all responsible. Educator or not, read this book: it is our North Star."

—**ROBIN D. G. KELLEY**, author of
Freedom Dreams: The Black Radical Imagination

WE WANT TO DO MORE THAN SURVIVE

ABOLITIONIST TEACHING AND THE PURSUIT OF EDUCATIONAL FREEDOM

BETTINA L. LOVE

Beacon Press ▪ Boston

BEACON PRESS
Boston, Massachusetts
www.beacon.org

Beacon Press books
are published under the auspices of
the Unitarian Universalist Association of Congregations.

23 22 21   8 7 (pbk.)
23 22 21 20   12 11 10 9 (hc.)

This book is printed on acid-free paper that meets the uncoated paper
ANSI/NISO specifications for permanence as revised in 1992.

Text design and composition by Kim Arney

Library of Congress Cataloging-in-Publication Data

Names: Love, Bettina L., author.
Title: We want to do more than survive : abolitionist teaching and the
pursuit of educational freedom / Bettina L. Love.
Description: Boston : Beacon Press, [2019] | Includes bibliographical
references and index.
Identifiers: LCCN 2018038260 (print) | LCCN 2018050423 (ebook) | ISBN
9780807069165 (ebook) | ISBN 9780807069158 (hardcover : acid-free paper)
| ISBN 9780807028346 (paperback : acid-free paper)
Subjects: LCSH: African Americans—Education. | Educational
equalization—United States. | Educational change—United States. |
Community and school—United States. | Education—Parent
participation—United States.
Classification: LCC LC2717 (ebook) | LCC LC2717 .L68 2019 (print) |
DDC 371.829/96073—dc23
LC record available at https://lccn.loc.gov/2018038260

My mission in life is not merely to survive, but to thrive; and to do so with some passion, some compassion, some humor, and some style.

—MAYA ANGELOU

CONTENTS

CHAPTER 1

"WE WHO ARE DARK"

What do we want? What is the thing we are after? . . . We want to be Americans, full-fledged Americans, with all the rights of other American citizens. But is that all? Do we want simply to be Americans? Once in a while through all of us there flashes some clairvoyance, some clear idea, of what America really is. We who are dark can see America in a way that white Americans cannot. And seeing our country thus, are we satisfied with its present goals and ideals?

—W. E. B. DU BOIS[1]

WE WHO ARE DARK. WE WHO ARE DARK. WE WHO ARE DARK. When I read Du Bois's words for the first time, they seemed to lift right off the page, as if they were meant expressly for me. Du Bois's indictment of America is plain and simple, yet at the same time shattering, because we as dark people see—which White Americans cannot—a country with enough promise to capture and hold four hundred years of freedom dreams while systematically attacking, reducing, and/or destroying each and every aspiration. So, what do we want, knowing what we know? What is this thing we are after? Although no one person is equipped or has the right to speak for millions, particularly on the issues of race and racism, there is one thing that I know with everything I am: we who are dark want to matter and live, not just to survive but to thrive. Matter not for recognition or acknowledgment but to create new systems and structures for educational, political, economic, and community freedom. It would mean we matter enough that our citizenship, and the rights that come with it, are never questioned, reduced, or taken away regardless of our birthplace or the amount of melanin in our skin. Mattering, citizenship, community sovereignty, and humanity go hand in hand with the ideas of democracy, liberty, and justice for all, which are the unalienable rights needed to thrive.

This book is about mattering, surviving, resisting, thriving, healing, imagining, freedom, love, and joy: all elements of abolitionist work and teaching. Abolitionist teaching is the practice of working in solidarity with communities of color while drawing on the imagination, creativity, refusal, (re)membering, visionary thinking, healing, rebellious spirit, boldness, determination, and subversiveness of abolitionists to eradicate injustice in and outside of schools.

To begin the work of abolitionist teaching and fighting for justice, the idea of mattering is essential in that you must matter enough to yourself, to your students, and to your students' community to fight. But for dark people, the very basic idea of mattering is sometimes hard to conceptualize when your country finds you disposable. How do you matter to a country that is at once obsessed with and dismissive about how it kills you? How do you matter to a country that would rather incarcerate you than educate you? How do you matter to a country that poisoned your child's drinking water? How do you matter to a country that sees your skin as a weapon? How do you matter to a country that steals your land, breaks treaty after treaty, and then calls you a savage? How do you matter to a country that tears families apart because of arbitrary lines that instill terror, violence, and geographical separation rather than a compassion for humanity? How do you matter to a country that will ban you because of how you pray and who you pray to? How do you matter to a country that ultimately only sees you as property or a commodity? How do you matter to a country that rips children out of the hands of their parents and locks them in dog cages for seeking a better life? How do you matter to a country that measures your knowledge against a "gap" it created? How do you matter to a country that labels you a "model minority" in order to fuel anti-Blackness? How do you matter to a country that would rather arm teachers with rocks than have courageous conversations with itself about gun control, eliminating guns, and White male rage? How do you matter to a country where the idea of "consent" seems alien to its conquering culture? How do you matter to a country where the president calls immigrants animals, particularly those from Mexico? How do you matter to a country where Betsy DeVos, a billionaire heiress and staunch advocate of privatizing public education, who refuses to protect our most vulnerable students in public schools, is the secretary of education? How do you matter to a country that is incapable of loving dark bodies and, therefore, incapable of loving you?

We who are dark are complex—we are more than our skin hues of Blacks and Browns. We intersect our moonlit darkness with our culture(s), language(s), race(s), gender(s), sexuality(ies), ability(ies), religion(s), and spirituality(ies). Our complicated identities cannot be discussed or examined in isolation from one another. These identity complexities, which create our multifaceted range of beings, must matter too.

Kimberlé Crenshaw refers to these multiple markers of identity as "intersectionality." Intersectionality is not just about listing and naming your identities—it is a necessary analytic tool to explain the complexities and the realities of discrimination and of power or the lack thereof, and how they intersect with identities. The idea of intersectionality is not new; Black women writers and thinkers throughout history, like Anna Julia Cooper, Audre Lorde, Angela Davis, Frances Beal, Patricia Hill Collins, and the women of the Combahee River Collective, articulated the need to discuss race and gender together, understanding that "multiple oppressions reinforce each other to create new categories of suffering."[2] Further, intersectionality cannot be conflated with diversity. "Diversity" is a catchall term that includes different types of people in terms of race, gender, sexuality, or religion within an organization, community, company, or school. "Intersectionality" is more than counting representation in a room or within a group; it is understanding community power, or its lack, and ensuring inclusivity in social justice movements. It is a way to build alliances in organizing for social change.

For example, there was a significant need for an intersectional lens when, in 1991, law professor Anita Hill accused US Supreme Court nominee Clarence Thomas of sexual harassment during his tenure as her boss at the US Department of Education and the Equal Employment Opportunity Commission. Many Americans, including many folx of color, did not believe Hill simply because she was a Black woman calling out a high-profile Black man. Thomas called the allegations a "high-tech lynching" to invoke Black male racial suffering and simultaneously erase Black women's history of racial and sexual trauma. Thomas's lynching comment caused people to view the case through the lens of race and racism, but only from a male perspective. His rhetorical maneuver painted Hill as a bitter Black woman trying to bring a Black man down like so many White people had done before. Thus, while diversity was present in the proceedings involving a Black man and a Black woman, both of them extremely accomplished, Thomas's male privilege, along with America's ignorance and outright disregard of Black women's own history of lynchings and sexual trauma due to assault, harassment, and rape, made it easy for America to ignore Hill's accusations. And even today, we see the "high-tech lynching" claim used to excuse Bill Cosby's numerous sexual assaults. Intersectionality would have allowed both race and Black women's history of sexual trauma to enter the conversation.

Sadly, in addition to Bill Cosby being a rapist, he is also a great example of someone who stood for racial uplift but not intersectional social justice; the two terms are often conflated. Cosby generously gave to historically Black colleges and universities and initiatives that supported the racial uplift of Black people, but his justice stopped there. The racial uplift of dark people is crucial, but that uplift cannot come at the expense of trans folx, folx with disabilities, or women.

Another useful example of the need for intersectionality can be seen in the pay discrepancies in the medical field. Male doctors make about $20,000 more per year than female doctors.[3] White male doctors make about $65,000 more than Black male doctors. Black female doctors make $25,000 less than White female doctors.[4] White male, Black male, and White female doctors all make more than Black female doctors. Black female doctors are paid less because of their race and their gender. Their pay is not an indication of skill level or education; it is an example of the intersections of discrimination.

In education, it is not well publicized that Black girls are suspended at a rate that is six times higher than that of their White female peers. In 2012, in New York City, fifty-three Black girls were expelled compared with zero White girls.[5] In every state in America, Black girls are more than twice as likely to be suspended from school as White girls.[6] And darker-skinned Black girls are suspended at a rate that is three times greater than those with lighter skin.[7] Research shows that these higher rates of suspension are not because of misbehavior (a determination that is incredibly subjective, especially when race is a part of the equation) but because of racist and sexist stereotypes that teachers and school officials hold against Black girls. For too many, suspension is a birthright of being young and Black.

In Monique W. Morris's book *Pushout: The Criminalization of Black Girls in School*, she documents how Black girls are branded "disruptive" or "defiant" by their teachers, then expelled or suspended because of such subjective labels.[8] Morris's book, as well as the work of many other activists and scholars, sparked a national conversation centered on Black girls who feel ignored and disrespected by their teachers and/or administrators, all while dealing with poverty, sexual abuse, emotional numbing, disabilities, low self-esteem, mental health issues, gender transitions, or the trials of simply being Black and a young girl trying to navigate adolescence. Morris argues that Black girls never get to be girls, a phenomenon she describes as "age compression," in which Black girls are seen as Black women, with all the stereotypes that go along with Black womanhood (e.g., hypersexual, loud, rude, and aggressive). By examining age compression of Black girls in school using intersectionality, we complicate the phenomenon and can ask important, unanswered questions: What does this school reality mean for Black girls who are a part of the LGBTQ community, Black girls who are Muslim, Black girls who are immigrants, Black girls who are disabled, and Black girls who are incarcerated or formerly incarcerated? What does this school reality mean for a Latinx girl who is queer, undocumented, and disabled? How do Black girls who are a combination of these identities deal with the complexities and the realities of discrimination, harassment, and violence? In this way, intersectionality not only provides a way in which to think about the communities we belong to but also a means to discuss all of our communities in ways that are inclusive of how oppression intersects our everyday lives inside and outside of school. Importantly, intersectionality does not ignore Black and Brown boys, who endure many similar issues; it merely adds complexity to our understandings of how institutions such as public schools are oppressive in different ways to different people.

Another timely example that highlights the need for intersectionality is the ridiculous proposal to arm teachers with guns. After the Marjory Stoneman Douglas High School shooting in Parkland, Florida, that killed seventeen people, President Donald Trump, other Republicans, and, of course, the National Rifle Association suggested that giving teachers guns would prevent school shootings. Not only is this a terrible idea for obvious reasons (e.g., the armed sheriff assigned to protect Stoneman Douglas High School did not enter the school while the gunman was inside), but the conversation about arming teachers was silent on race and disability.

Over the past few years, we have watched video after video of dark children being assaulted in classrooms by teachers and school police officers. School officials grossly and racially punish dark students. The American Civil Liberties Union reported that "students of color, students with disabilities, and students of color with disabilities are more likely to be funneled into the criminal justice system for behavior that may warrant supportive interventions or a trip to the principal's office, not a criminal record."[9] Thus, on a day-to-day basis, arming teachers with guns would threaten the lives of dark students and dark students with disabilities more than a mass school shooter, particularly because data tell us that mass shootings are rare in urban schools. Policy agendas devoid of intersectionality do not allow questions and dialogues that reflect the lives of the people who will be impacted by policy. As preposterous as the conversation is around arming teachers, the discussion shows that racial and disability analyses are necessary for dialogues about schools because schools are inherently violent to dark children and children with disabilities.

Intersectionality also allows educators to dialogue around a set of questions that will lead them to a better sense of their students' full selves, their students' challenges, the grace and beauty that is needed to juggle multiple identities seamlessly, and how schools perpetuate injustice. When teachers shy away from intersectionality, they shy away from ever fully knowing their students' humanity and the richness of their identities. Mattering cannot happen if identities are isolated and students cannot be their full selves.

SO, WHAT IS MATTERING?

I am certain that dark people have never truly mattered in this country except as property and labor. However, we have mattered to our communities, to our families, and to ourselves. Our impact on this country, whether it is recognized or not, is where mattering rests; it is where thriving rests. Mattering is civics because it is the quest for humanity. I do not mean civics narrowly defined as voting, paying taxes, and knowing how the government works; instead, I am referring to something much deeper: the practice of abolitionist teaching rooted in the internal desire we all have for freedom, joy, restorative justice (restoring humanity, not just rules), and to matter to ourselves, our community, our family, and our country with the profound understanding that we must "demand the impossible"[10] by refusing injustice and the disposability of dark children. Demanding the impossible means we understand that racism, sexism, homophobia, transphobia, Islamophobia, classism, mass incarceration, and US Immigration and Customs Enforcement (ICE) are protected systems that will not be dismantled because we ask; they will be dismantled because we fight, demanding what they said was impossible, remembering through the words of Angela Y. Davis that "freedom is a constant struggle."[11]

Mattering has always been the job of Black, Brown, and Indigenous folx since the "human hierarchy" was invented to benefit Whites by rationalizing racist ideas of biological racial inferiority to "those Americans who believe that they are White."[12] Being a person of color is a civic project because your relationship to America, sadly, is a fight in order to matter, to survive, and one day thrive. In his book *Between the World and Me*, Ta-Nehisi Coates explains to his son, "The entire narrative of this country argues against the truth of who you are."[13] America's legacy of oppression and dispossession of dark people is in large part met with the ethos of "We Shall Overcome," "Sí Se Puede," and "We Gon' Be Alright." This is not to say that we have not resisted, rioted, and rebelled, rightfully so and with righteous rage. It is these acts of rebellion that have allowed us to create a collective identity and, therefore, build schools, educate our children, use the church as a place of worship and community building, gather the best legal minds to argue for basic human rights, take to the streets as a demonstration of our commitment, and withdraw or withhold our money from companies and institutions that demean and deny us. It is these acts that have allowed us to produce beautiful, visceral, and eloquent literature, photography, visual art, and films that explain and endure our suffering, soundscapes for all to enjoy (but which only those in the struggle can feel and heal from), body movements that express pain and joy simultaneously, food that can only be made from love, and a joy that cannot be replicated outside of the dark body. We have created in the void, defiant of the country's persistent efforts to kill and commodify us. Finding ways to matter.

WELCOME STRUGGLE

For those of us who are dark, our lives are entrenched, whether we like it or not, in creating what Dr. Martin Luther King Jr. called a "beloved community," a community that strives for economic, housing, racial, health, and queer justice and citizenship for all. This is the work of mattering to one another. It is the work of pursuing freedom. It is the work of our survival, and how we will one day thrive together. It is how dark folx in this country have always mattered to each other, by attempting to carve out, on the edges of total degradation, common goals for justice, liberation, liberty, and freedom that inspire and make this country better for *all*. We have not always agreed on the methods of liberation, but the work has never ceased. The approach of Dr. King, often guided by civil rights activist and strategist Bayard Rustin, was one of nonviolence, coalition building, and courageous acts of resistance for social change. Ella Baker joined King and Rustin in their nonviolent approach but insisted that the more sustainable method was robust grassroots organizing, which cultivated civic and community leaders from within. The Black Panther Party fought for liberation by policing the police, preaching self-determination, and serving their communities through social and educational programming such as health clinics and food-justice programs. Political activist and scholar Angela Davis's mandate for fighting injustice is systemic change by way of mass movements for community sovereignty. None of these approaches is new or removed from the long history of abolitionist envisioning, mobilizing, and revolting against racial oppression. Indeed, these multiple methods remind us of the profound words of Michael Hames-García: "The very fact of freedom's incompleteness (no one is free so long as others remain unfree) necessitates action directed at changing society. Freedom, therefore, is ultimately a practice, rather than a possession or a state of being."[14] *To want freedom is to welcome struggle.* This idea is fundamental to abolitionist teaching. We are not asking for struggle; we just understand that justice will not happen without it.

When you understand how hard it is to fight for educational justice, you know that there are no shortcuts and no gimmicks; you know this to be true deep in your soul, which brings both frustration and determination. Educational justice is going to take people power, driven by the spirit and ideas of the folx who have done the work of antiracism before: abolitionists. The fact that dark people are tasked with the work of dismantling these centuries-old oppressions is a continuation of racism. Toni Morrison once said, "The function, the very serious function of racism is distraction. It keeps you from doing your work. It keeps you explaining, over and over again, your reason for being."[15] This endless, and habitually thankless, job of radical collective freedom-building is an act of survival, but we who are dark want to do more than survive: we want to thrive. A life of survival is not really living.

REFORM AIN'T JUSTICE

Education is an industry that is driven and financially backed by the realities that dark children and their families just survive. It is Teach for America's mantra: spend two years in an inner city or rural school with poor and/or dark children and help them survive. Individuals with little to no experience are tasked with working in struggling schools that were designed to fail (e.g., they are underfunded, with high teacher burnout, tests that punish students, and low-quality teachers) and given only two years—if they can make it that long—to "make a difference," when hundreds more qualified have tried and failed before them. These educational parasites need dark children to be underserved and failing, which supports their feel-good, quick-fix, gimmicky narrative and the financial reason for their existence. Education reform is big business, just like prisons. Creating the narrative that dark people are criminals to justify locking them up for profit is no different from continuously reminding the American public that there is an educational achievement gap while conveniently never mentioning America's role in creating the gap. Both prisons and schools create a narrative of public outrage and fear that dark bodies need saving from themselves. The two industries play off each other, and America believes that criminality and low achievement go hand in hand. The four major testing companies—Pearson Education, Educational Testing Service, Houghton Mifflin Harcourt, and McGraw-Hill—make $2 billion a year in revenue while spending $20 million a year lobbying for more mandated student assessments.[16] Prisons bring in $70 billion a year in revenue, and its industry spends $45 million a year lobbying to keep people incarcerated and for longer sentences.[17]

Education reformers take up space in urban schools offering nothing more than survival tactics to children of color in the forms of test-taking skills, acronyms, grit labs, and character education. The barriers of racism, discrimination, concentrated poverty, and access to college—persistent, structural barriers—cannot be eradicated by tweaking the system or making adjustments. We must struggle together not only to reimagine schools but to build new schools that we are taught to believe are impossible: schools based on intersectional justice, antiracism, love, healing, and joy. This book is about that struggle and the possibilities of committing ourselves to an abolitionist pursuit to educational freedom—freedom, not reform. Abolitionist teaching is built on the creativity, imagination, boldness, ingenuity, and rebellious spirit and methods of abolitionists to demand and fight for an education system where all students are thriving, not simply surviving.

I know as an educator that this task seems daunting and overwhelming in an already taxing mission, but courage and vision are required. Abolitionist teaching is choosing to engage in the struggle for educational justice knowing that you have the ability and human right to refuse oppression and refuse to oppress others, mainly your students. What does this approach look like in the classroom and beyond? Teachers working with community groups in solidarity to address issues impacting their students and their students' communities. Reimagining and rewriting curriculums with local and national activists to provide students with not only examples of resistance but also strategies of resistance. Protecting and standing in solidarity with immigrant children and their families. Joining pro-immigrant community organizations in the fight for rights for all. Knowing that freedom is impossible without women and queer leaders being the thinkers and doers of abolitionist movements. Engaging in civics education that teaches direct action and civil disobedience while incorporating the techniques of the millennial freedom-fighting generation, such as social media, impactful hashtags, and online petitions.

Abolitionist teaching is refusing to take part in zero-tolerance policies and the school-to-prison pipeline. Demanding restorative justice in our schools as the only schoolwide or districtwide approach to improving school culture. Refusing the idea that children do not need recess and insisting that all children need to play. Abolitionist teaching ensures that students feel safe in schools and that schools are not perpetrators of violence toward the very students they are supposed to protect. Abolitionist teaching is calling out your fellow teachers who degrade and diminish dark children and do not think dark children matter—we must demand that they leave the profession; we have to call them out. Abolitionist teaching stands in solidarity with parents and fellow teachers opposing standardized testing, English-only education, racist teachers, arming teachers with guns, and turning schools into prisons. Abolitionist teaching supports and teaches from the space that Black Lives Matter, all Black Lives Matter, and affirms Black folx' humanity.

Abolitionist teaching asks educators to acknowledge and accept America and its policies as anti-Black, racist, discriminatory, and unjust and to be in solidarity with dark folx and poor folx fighting for their humanity and fighting to move beyond surviving. To learn the sociopolitical landscape of their students' communities through a historical, intersectional justice lens. To abandon teaching gimmicks like "grit" that present the experiences of dark youth as ahistorical and further pathologize them and evoke collective freedom dreaming. These dreams are spaces of love, solidarity, and resiliency, as we demand what seems impossible from a place of love and joy. While we do not forget injustice, we are focused instead on love, well-being, and joy and refuse to be oppressed any longer. Lastly, teachers must embrace theories such as critical race theory, settler colonialism, Black feminism, dis/ability, critical race studies, and other critical theories that have the ability to interrogate anti-Blackness and frame experiences with injustice, focusing the moral compass toward a North Star that is ready for a long and dissenting fight for educational justice. These theories additionally help in understanding that educational justice can happen only through a simultaneous fight for economic justice, racial justice, housing justice, environmental justice, religious justice, queer justice, trans justice, citizenship justice, and disability justice.

DO WE REALLY LOVE ALL CHILDREN?

To achieve the goals of abolitionist teaching, we must demand the impossible and employ a radical imagination focused on intersectional justice through community building and grassroots organizing.

To even begin to attack our destructive and punitive educational system, pedagogies that promote social justice must have teeth. They must move beyond feel-good language and gimmicks to help educators understand and recognize America and its schools as spaces of Whiteness, White rage, and White supremacy, all of which function to terrorize students of color. For example, too much of the field of education is filled with quick fixes or slogans (e.g., No Excuses), gimmicks (e.g., grit), best practices (e.g., benchmarking), and professional developments (e.g., Understanding Poverty) that focus on dark students through the lenses of daily struggles with trauma, gaps in learning, poverty, hunger, and language barriers. Each fix falls short precisely because it fails to acknowledge how these struggles are direct consequences of injustice.

Education research is crowded with studies that acknowledge dark children's pain but never the source of their pain, the legacy that pain has left, or how that pain can be healed. I have seen professional development sessions titled "The Crisis in Black Education," "The Problem with Black Boys," and "Addressing a Poverty Mindset." These types of workshops White-splain Black folx' challenges to White folx but rarely discuss the topics of redlining, housing discrimination, White flight, gentrification, police brutality, racial health disparities, and high unemployment, problems that are not due to low levels of education but to the racism discussed.[18] Teaching strategies and education reform models must offer more than educational survival tactics to dark children—test-taking skills, acronyms, character education, No Child Left Behind, Race to the Top, charter schools, school choice. They need to be rooted in an abolitionist praxis that, with urgency, embraces what seems impossible: education for collective dignity and human power for justice.

Teachers who say they are deeply concerned about social justice or that they "love all children" but cannot say the words "Black Lives Matter" have no real understanding of what social justice is and what it truly means to love, find joy, and appreciate their students and their students' culture. For the past ten years I have taught future teachers at the collegiate level. In 2016, right after the election of Trump, one of my White students, who "loves all children," posted a picture on In-stagram with her boyfriend wearing a sweater that read "All I Want for Christmas Is Hillary's Emails," captioned "#buildthatwall." Through-out the semester this student said and wrote all the right things to demonstrate a belief in social justice and an assumption that all stu-dents could learn, that diversity was important, and that community building was a vital part of education. However, moving theory to practice was shattered with that one post. In actuality, for most stu-dents—not all, but most—one course focused on social justice cannot undo a lifetime of racist thinking and of learning in racial isolation. My point here is not to endorse Hillary Clinton—especially since many of her policies were anti-Black—but to highlight how a future educator can engage the language of justice and culturally relevant teaching, while webbed to a disposition that is harmful to all students.

In reality, many of these teachers who "love all children" are deeply entrenched in racism, transphobia, classism, rigid ideas of gen-der, and Islamophobia. These teachers do not belong in classrooms with dark children or even White children because antidarkness can happen without dark children in the room. Antidarkness is the social disregard for dark bodies and the denial of dark people's existence and humanity.[19] When White students attend nearly all-White schools, intentionally removed from America's darkness to reinforce White dominance, that is antidarkness. When dark people are presented in school curriculums as unfortunate circumstances of history, that is antidarkness. When schools are filled with White faces in positions of authority and dark faces in the school's help staff, that is antidark-ness. The idea that dark people have had no impact on history or the progress of mankind is one of the foundational ideas of White supremacy. Denying dark people's existence and contributions to hu-man progress relegates dark folx to being takers and not cocreators of history or their lives. If we are being truly honest, if a teacher be-lieves Mexicans are "animals," that teacher cannot teach Mexican children. Simply said, a teacher cannot support hateful rhetoric about dark children and their families and still teach them with kindness, love, and care and see the beauty in that child's culture.

Simply put, many of our schools function as spaces of dark suffering. Education researcher Michael Dumas argues that schools operate as spaces of "racial suffering" because "educational access and opportunity seems increasingly (and even intentionally) elusive" to dark children.[20] To understand schools as sites of dark suffering is to understand how antidarkness works in the day-to-day lives of both dark and White children. Antidarkness in our schools cannot be remedied by advocating for charter schools, No Child Left Behind (President George W. Bush's education reform policy), the Common Core, or Race to the Top (President Barack Obama's education reform policy); the perpetual suffering dark families endure in yearning for an education for their children is the elucidation of survival, the conundrum of a dark reality. What is astonishing is that through all the suffering the dark body endures, there is joy, Black joy. I do not mean the type of fabricated and forced joy found in a Pepsi commercial; I am talking about joy that originates in resistance, joy that is discovered in making a way out of no way, joy that is uncovered when you know how to love yourself and others, joy that comes from releasing pain, joy that is generated in music and art that puts words and/or images to your life's greatest challenges and pleasures, and joy in teaching from a place of resistance, agitation, purpose, justice, love, and mattering.

This book is about struggle and the possibilities of committing ourselves to an abolitionist approach to educational freedom, not reform, built on criticality civics, joy, theory, love, refusal, creativity, community, and, ultimately, mattering. Because through flashes of clairvoyance, present goals and ideals reveal that what we who are dark want is to matter to this country and thrive as full-fledged Americans, with all the rights of White American citizens.

CHAPTER 2

EDUCATIONAL SURVIVAL

Survival: The state or fact of continuing to live or exist, typically in spite of an accident, ordeal, or difficult circumstances.

—OXFORD ENGLISH DICTIONARY

American history is longer, larger, more various, more beautiful, and more terrible than anything anyone has ever said about it.

—JAMES BALDWIN[1]

I STARTED MY TEACHING CAREER MORE THAN FIFTEEN YEARS ago in Homestead, Florida, not far from Everglades National Park and Turkey Point. In 2016, a nuclear power plant leaked dangerous water waste into Biscayne Bay, ultimately polluting nearby drinking supplies. Like most teachers, I did not live near my school; I lived in Miami, approximately forty miles away. I was young and wanted nothing more than to call my family in cold upstate New York to casually remind them that I was living in tropical Miami, just miles from the beach. However, Monday through Friday, and on some weekends, I drove down what felt like the never-ending highway of US 1 and entered what seemed to be a different world unfamiliar to most. It was my first time living in a place where saying the word "diversity" felt genuine. There were so many shades of dark children who spoke with the tongue of my ancestors unknown to me. Although my school was filled with mostly Black students, the halls were packed with teachers, administrators, and students from Haiti, Mexico, Colombia, Cuba, and Guatemala. The school printed permission slips in three languages: English, Spanish, and Haitian Creole. As diverse as the school was, and still is, its diversity was held together by poverty. The school was a perfect example of the need for intersectionality in the field of education, of how race, ethnicity, nationality, and class intersect and leave students living and learning in enclaves of racial (dark) and economic isolation.

Back in 2003, when I was teaching second and third grade, I did not have the sociopolitical awareness or language to know that I was witnessing and participating in dark suffering and the educational survival complex. I remember feeling overwhelmed with confusion the first time I learned that many of my students had never gone to South Beach in Miami, or that a few were repeating the third grade because their parents were migrant workers, so they never completed a full year of school in the same year. A student of a migrant family would start at our school, leave in the middle of the year, and then return after their parents' seasonal work had ended. The flux of work coupled with the high-stakes testing of No Child Left Behind perpetually and deliberately did, in fact, leave these students to flounder; to be blunt, they were not even playing in the same game as their peers who lived on the pristine roads of South Florida.

A good number of my students came from poor working families. These parents went to work every day at the bottom of the US wage distribution; they worked simply, at best, to survive. The reality is that "our political economy is structured to create poverty and inequality."[2] Schools reflect our political economy. The fact that schools are funded by local property taxes ensures that students who live in poor communities receive an education that will maintain, and, in fact, widen the gap between the über-rich, the rich, the rapidly shrinking middle class, the working poor, and the poor. This system renders schools ineffective in providing poor students any type of real social mobility. Schools in higher-income districts or rich enclaves are well-resourced, have high-quality teachers, and have low teacher turnover. In addition, the Parent Teacher Associations of affluent schools work to ensure that extracurricular activities, community initiatives, and field trips are offered to the already privileged.

To put some real numbers to the lives of average families, in 2017, 95 percent of wealth created went directly into the pockets of the top 1 percent of society.[3] Meanwhile, the median income for a family of four was $54,000, with $16,000 in credit card debt, more than $172,806 in home mortgages, $28,535 in car loans, and just under $50,000 in student loans.[4] This economic state is what our country calls the middle class—folx in debt, barely hanging on, living paycheck to paycheck. This perpetual state of financial precariousness is only exacerbated when you are dark, poor, and living in isolation.

In terms of race, a 2014 study found that the wealth gap between White and Black families had widened to its highest levels since 1989.[5] The children of Black families that do reach the middle class have a more difficult time maintaining that status, much less achieving more than their parents. For example, Black college graduates are twice as likely to experience unemployment as their White counterparts. College-educated Hispanics were hit hard by the collapse of the housing market: their net worth crashed 72 percent between 2007 and 2013.[6]

Although these reported statistics paint a bleak picture, they do not even come close to capturing the lives of my former students in South Florida. My students were far from middle class; the median household income in that area for 2003 was roughly $36,850, with 28.3 percent of people living below the poverty line ($19,500 for a family of four). Today the poverty line is roughly $24,250, with racism and sexism still at the core of poverty, woven into the fabric of the US. According to 2016 US Census data, women were 35 percent more likely to live in poverty than men.[7] Of the 16.9 million women living in poverty, 45.7 percent live in extreme poverty, with an income at or below 50 percent of the federal poverty level.[8] It is no coincidence that women of color and their children make up a vast majority of women living in poverty.

Education researchers know that without a long-term strategy to eradicate the causes of racial and economic isolation—such as discrimination, predatory lending, housing displacement, the gender wage gap, rising healthcare costs, and unemployment (which leads to the 99 percent being no better than indentured servants to the 1 percent)—"heroic attempts to restructure schools or to introduce new pedagogical techniques in the classroom will be difficult to sustain."[9] No type of pedagogy, however effective, can single-handedly remove the barriers of racism, discrimination, homophobia, segregation, Islamophobia, homelessness, access to college, and concentrated poverty, but antiracist pedagogy combined with grassroots organizing can prepare students and their families to demand the impossible in the fight for eradicating these persistent and structural barriers. Pedagogy should work in tandem with students' own knowledge of their community and grassroots organizations to push forward new ideas for social change, not just be a tool to enhance test scores or grades. Pedagogy, regardless of its name, is useless without teachers dedicated to challenging systemic oppression with intersectional social justice.

To that end, the state of Florida labeled my school a failing school, an "F" school. In Florida, individual schools are given letter grades based on Florida's Standards Assessment, with the Florida Comprehensive Assessment Test (FCAT) being a significant portion of the grade. Yearly, these grades are released in the newspaper for all to see. As a first-year teacher, I was confused about what my job was as an educator. What were my priorities? I felt as though my job centered on teaching to the test to raise test scores so the school would not be taken over by the state or closed down. At times it felt like our students' low test scores threatened our ability to keep our jobs, our homes, our livelihoods. It was also the first time in my life I was making enough money to cover my bills. I didn't want to give that security up, even though I was underpaid. I was struggling to remember why I became a teacher, and the students were struggling with the purpose of it all. We were all trying to survive.

As a parent, I cannot imagine the frustration, anger, and hopelessness of waking up your child every morning to attend a failing school. But what about the students? What does it mean to walk into a building every day thinking the school is failing not because of teachers or administrators, nor a sociopolitical history of dark communities being intentionally destabilized, terrorized, and put into a carceral state, but because of your dark skin? A good number of my students in Homestead, especially those whose second language was English—language being a critical component of a person's identity—had failed the FCAT multiple times because it was administered in English. Failing a test because your language is deemed inferior communicates a message about your identity and ideas of who is and what is smart.

Some of my students were repeating the third grade for the second or third time. The FCAT did not measure their intelligence; it just served as another reminder that their darkness and language were not valued in a country that may require the completion of a Spanish-language class to graduate from high school but condemns you for speaking Spanish as your first language. This paradox is what it means for your culture to be invisible and visible at the same time. Surrounded by inequalities, dark students begin to think that dark suffering is normal. How do children with the world in front of them make peace with their suffering? How and should they make peace with their suffering? Faced with these issues, I was lost as a new teacher.

As I relate my experiences, and put the pieces together after all these years, the words of James Baldwin seem appropriate and clairvoyant in regard to the lives of my students and me: "This innocent country set you down in a ghetto in which, in fact, it intended that you should perish. . . . You were born into a society which spelled out with brutal clarity, and in as many ways as possible, that you were a worthless human being."[10] These dark families were "casualties of America's war on the vulnerable."[11]

Langston Hughes's poem "Harlem" begins by asking the question: "What happens to a dream deferred?"[12] My students were smart, funny, kind, hardworking, and hopeful, with dreams of their own. However, my students were physically, emotionally, financially, geographically, and educationally trapped. Telling them they could be whatever they wanted to be was simply a lie, and they knew it. The barriers of race, language, and class predetermined their place in the world. My students were angry and I understood this anger firsthand. I grew up in the inner city of Rochester, New York, where I attended subpar schools. I was able to flee my own version of Harlem on a college basketball scholarship, but I arrived academically unprepared and broke.

Ultimately, my students in Homestead pushed me to become a better teacher by prompting me to ask myself difficult questions about our existence as dark people and my role in helping us unpack our trapped shared fates. Over the course of my time there, which was not long because I left to enter a PhD program, I did not move beyond the surface of teaching educational survival skills—high-stakes standardized testing, assessments, grades, character education—because the fate of my students had little relation to such lessons; it was their lives, their humanity, their dignity playing out in that school every day. As I write this book, I am expected to humanize my students, write vignettes about my educational experiences that highlighted ups and downs in the classroom, but the simple truth is, my students and I were merely trying to survive. We all carried the inflicted weight of America's dark suffering.

Looking back now, I see my first year as a teacher was riddled with insecurities. Although my students were new to me, I felt as though I knew them all personally because there were pieces of me inside each of them. I knew the shape of their noses, the fullness of their lips. I shared with them what it feels like on a hot summer day to watch your skin made darker by the kiss of the sun, but I also know that our beautiful skin functions as a biological, ebony-colored tattoo that labels our bodies and our spirits as disposable to those who produce and consume racist ideas. I heard the whispered racist comments about dark children in the halls of a building filled with the elusive hopes and dreams of racial progress. I personally witnessed educators lower their expectations for students of color while insisting they were doing what was best for their students. I knew the face and crooked smile of a child who walks into a school building every day determined to be the extraordinary, magical Negro who proves teachers wrong about his or her intellectual abilities, and I knew the face of anger and anguish of a child who has analyzed with great complexity the rigged and unjust system of public education for dark children, who has experienced suffering and sits in a class infuriated by the circumstances that dictate his or her life. I was watching, living, and teaching education for survival, at best, without an understanding of why I could not get out of survival mode. I did not truly understand what came before me that set the stage for the dark suffering I was experiencing, which, while contextually different from my own childhood as a little Black girl in upstate New York, felt so familiar: growing up dark.

WHITE RAGE

The conditions that preserve dark suffering are the result of hundreds of years and multiple continents' commitment to creating and maintaining destructive, insidious, racist ideals that uphold White supremacy and anti-Blackness. The field of education is anchored in White rage, especially public education. We like to think that education is untouched by White supremacy, White rage, and anti-Blackness, that educators are somehow immune to perpetuating dark suffering. But education from the outset was built on White supremacy, anti-Blackness, and sexism. America's first public schools, often called grammar schools, were only for White, wealthy males. And over time, when any group outside of the established norm fought for the right to educate their children, particularly by way of their culture and/or language, they were met with White rage. Native American children were taken away from their families and put into boarding schools (such as Pennsylvania's Carlisle Indian Industrial School), African American children were told second-class schooling was fine by way of "separate but equal," California school codes excluded Asian American children from public schools, and in 1855, California required that all school instruction be conducted in English.

When the United States invaded Puerto Rico in 1898 and took over the country in what former president Ulysses S. Grant called "the most unjust war ever waged by a stronger against a weaker nation,"[13] Spanish was replaced with English and teachers were brought from America to teach Puerto Rican children. Education is one of the primary tools used to maintain White supremacy and anti-immigrant hate. Teachers entering the field of education must know this history, acknowledge this history, and understand why it matters in the present-day context of education, White rage, and dark suffering.

In discussions of the South, oftentimes, Florida is not included. Conversations about slavery, Jim Crow, and the civil rights movement primarily focus on Georgia, Mississippi, Louisiana, and Alabama, because many significant court cases and historic marches and protests took place in these states. But Florida's history is important to understanding present-day injustices (the killings of Trayvon Martin and Jordan Davis, the "stand your ground" law) and my former school.

You cannot discuss White supremacy without considering White rage. Historian Carol Anderson, author of *White Rage: The Unspoken Truth of Our Racial Divide*, argues, "The trigger of White rage, inevitably, is Black advancement. It is not the mere presence of Black people that is the problem; rather it is Blackness with ambition, with drive, with purpose, with aspirations, and with demands for full and equal citizenship."[14] A devastating example of White rage, which is always present, festering, and plotting, occurred in the town of Ocoee, Florida, on November 2, 1920. The region was a stronghold of the Ku Klux Klan. According to reports, until at least 1959, a sign hung at the town's line that read "Dogs and Negroes Not Welcomed."[15] Ocoee was also considered a sundown town, described by historian and author James W. Loewen as an "organized jurisdiction that for decades kept African Americans or other groups from living in it and was thus 'all-White' on purpose."[16] White rage erupted when John Moses Cheney, a white judge who supported efforts to register Black voters to win his campaign, and two Black businessmen, Mose Norman and Julius "July" Perry, publicly encouraged Black folx to vote. Perry "encouraged young blacks to be educated and stand up for themselves as first-class citizens."[17] As Black folx arrived at the polls on Election Day, they were met by a growing White mob. When the dust settled, sixty

Black citizens had been killed and their property destroyed for having ambition, drive, and purpose: for mattering. Perry was lynched for daring to matter.

Almost sixty years later, on December 17, 1979, and 250 miles south down Florida's turnpike in Miami, Arthur McDuffie, a Black former Marine, ran a red light on his motorcycle and led four White police officers on an eight-minute high-speed chase. When the police finally stopped him, they beat him into a coma. He died four days later at a nearby hospital. The officers were charged with manslaughter and tampering with evidence. Due to fear of an uprising, the trial was moved to Tampa, where an all-White, all-male jury found the four officers not guilty. Miles away in Miami, a city of dark folx tired of being collectively punished and disempowered, people took to the streets in protest, which quickly escalated into a riot. Dr. Martin Luther King Jr. once said, "A riot is the language of the unheard." For three days in Miami, dark folx screamed at the top of their lungs but to deaf ears. In a city divided and enraged—darkness on one side, Whiteness on the other—eighteen people died and over four hundred were injured. More than 3,500 National Guard officers flooded the streets. In the days following the uprising, the police officers responsible for McDuffie's death were reinstated after the Miami Fraternal Order of Police threatened a walkout.

While the McDuffie incident made national news, many similar instances of White Rage in Florida went unnoticed. Just one year earlier, in 1978, a White state trooper sexually molested an eleven-year-old Black girl. He received no jail time. That same year, an off-duty police officer working as a security guard shot and killed a twenty-two-year-old Black man. The officer faced no jail time. In 1979, detectives mistakenly served a search warrant at the home of a retired Black educator, who was then seriously injured in a struggle with police. No criminal charges were brought against the officers. Janet Reno, then the state's attorney for Miami-Dade County, upheld White rage by presiding over all of these cases. Black leaders demanded her removal from office, to no avail. Thirteen years later, President Bill Clinton nominated Reno to become the first woman to serve as United States attorney general. Reno's appointment came after two other female nominees withdrew (both were found to have employed undocumented workers).

In 2005, with the financial support and influence of the National Rifle Association (NRA), and in a country that had spent centuries criminalizing dark bodies, Florida passed its "stand your ground" law. The law was written to protect White rage and to uphold the power of conservative state legislators and private companies such as Walmart, America's largest seller of guns. Conservative lawmakers, the NRA, and Walmart were all members of the America Legislative Exchange Council, or ALEC, the organization that fought to expand the scope of the "castle doctrine" law, which allowed for violent self-defense in the home. The stand your ground law moved "home-defense principles into the streets."[18] In short, stand your ground gave immunity to White rage, the same White rage that has repeatedly and systematically kidnapped and killed dark children.

In 1955, Emmett Till, a fourteen-year-old Black boy from Chicago, was visiting his relatives in Money, Mississippi. The eighth grader was kidnapped and beaten to death for allegedly flirting with a White woman, Carolyn Bryant. Her husband, Roy Bryant, and his half-brother, J. W. Milam, brutally beat Emmett and then shot him in the head. His body was found days later in the Tallahatchie River. An all-White, all-male jury acquitted both men even after they admitted to kidnapping Emmett. In 2008, Carolyn Bryant, speaking to Timothy B. Tyson for his book on Emmett's death, admitted that Emmett never "grabbed her around the waist and uttered obscenities," which she had asserted under oath on the witness stand.[19] She later said in the same interview: "Nothing that boy did could ever justify what happened to him."[20]

White rage also claimed Addie Mae Collins (ten years old), Cynthia Wesley (fourteen), Carole Robertson (fourteen), and Denise McNair (eleven), the four girls killed in the bombing of the Sixteenth Street Baptist Church in Birmingham, Alabama, in 1963. Four Klan members placed fifteen sticks of dynamite underneath the front steps of the church and lit the fuse. These men were not charged with murder until 1977. Two were convicted and sent to prison in 2002, almost forty years after the bombing. The accounts of these children and their murderers are blatant, violent examples of this country's deep investment in White rage, in turn empowered by an (in)justice system that renders this nation a superpredator.

The United States has a long history of passing laws that protect Whites when they kill, torture, and displace dark people. The slave codes of the 1700s and 1800s allowed White men to kill Black people with impunity. The Indian Removal Act of 1830 killed thousands of Native Americans by forcefully removing them from their land in the Deep South to make room for White settlers who would become slaveholders. After Reconstruction, Jim Crow laws were enacted to maintain racial segregation and White rage. According to a report by the Equal Justice Initiative, between 1877 and 1950, nearly four thousand Black men, women, and children were lynched.[21] During World War II, Japanese Americans were forcibly taken to internment camps. The federal government apologized and disbursed over $36 million in reparations to 82,219 Japanese Americans.[22] In the summer of 2018, the US government labeled individuals seeking asylum along the US–Mexico border as criminals and placed their children in government foster care; some were put in cages. From October 1, 2017, to May 31, 2018, the government took more than 2,700 children from their families.[23] These horrific practices—lynchings, shootings, separating families, and beatings—were all protected by the US (in)justice superpredator system.

My experiences teaching in Florida represent just one statewide example of dark suffering at the hands of White rage. Backward-mapping Florida's history of White rage, in conversation with the US as a whole, provides some of the sociopolitical context needed to understand how George Zimmerman was free to shoot and kill unarmed teenager Trayvon Martin in Sanford, Florida, in 2012. That night, Trayvon was simply walking with a bag of Skittles and a can of iced tea in a gated community, which he had visited several times before, when the superpredator, White rage, took his life. Jurors at Zimmerman's trial were informed that Trayvon's killer had the right to stand his ground; no instructions were given regarding Trayvon's right to defend himself. Zimmerman was found not guilty.

Less than a year after Trayvon's murder, seventeen-year-old Jordan Davis was shot and killed at a gas station in Florida for playing loud rap music and not *obeying* a White man's command to turn his music down. Michael Dunn fired ten bullets into Jordan's SUV, almost killing Jordan's friends in the backset. After he fired those fatal shots, Dunn and his fiancée drove off, ordered pizza, walked their dog, and never called the police. Dunn's first trial resulted in a mistrial, but he was eventually convicted of first-degree murder and attempted murder. He will spend the rest of his life in prison, while Jordan's parents mourn their son for the rest of their lives. Trayvon and Jordan, like all dark children, had dreams. Their dreams were destroyed by White rage, rage that is endorsed, celebrated, and profited from in our schools because dark children are educated only to survive.

EDUCATIONAL SURVIVAL COMPLEX

Most dark suffering does not make the nightly news or our social media posts. If we are honest, most dark suffering goes unnoticed by too many Americans, but America's educational history is overrun with dark suffering. Native American boarding schools, school segregation, English-only instruction, *Brown v. Board of Education*, No Child Left Behind, school choice, charter schools, character education, Race to the Top . . . all have been components of an educational system built on the suffering of students of color. I call this the educational survival complex, in which students are left learning to merely survive, learning how schools mimic the world they live in, thus making schools a training site for a life of exhaustion.

This reality makes it difficult to digest the dark suffering that goes on in our schools because we want to believe that our schools can repair the sins of our nation. To mitigate their suffering and uphold Whiteness, dark families are given one short-sighted, often racist education reform model after another. First, the racist educational survival complex snatched Native American children away from their parents for religious and cultural conversion—nothing short of cultural and linguistic genocide. They established English-only schools. The racist educational survival complex told dark families that schools were "separate but equal." More than a lie, it was a legal tactic to maintain White superiority as Black folx demanded to matter. Next came the racial experiment of desegregating schools. Legal scholar Derrick Bell argued that Black folx would have been better served if the court had ruled differently in *Brown v. Board of Education* and enforced the "equal" part of "separate but equal." W. E. B. Du Bois made a similar argument in 1935; he proclaimed, "Negro children needed neither segregated schools nor mixed schools. What they need is education."[24]

Before the landmark decision of *Brown* in 1954, Black schools were proud institutions that "provided Black communities with cohesion and leadership."[25] Though Black schools' facilities and books were inferior to their White counterparts, the education they provided was not. In oral-history interviews, Black teachers reflecting on Black schools before *Brown* constantly made remarks like, "Black schools were places where order prevailed, where teachers commanded respect, and where parents supported teachers." Educating Black children was viewed as the collective responsibility of the community. Schools were the anchors for the Black community, and teachers were leaders inside and outside school walls. Schools represented spaces of solidarity, places to build power amid White rage. Schools were the foundation of moving toward thriving. The educational survival complex ensured that after *Brown*, Black folx would remain unable to thrive. White rage and White flight after *Brown* left Blacks in the inner cities in racial and economic isolation as Whites moved to the suburbs, thereby excluding dark people from employment, housing, higher property values (which help create generational wealth), and educational opportunities, while manufacturing imaginary school zone lines, which ensured that dark children could never attend schools with their White children. As schools desegregated, more than thirty-eight thousand Black teachers and principals lost their jobs due to the closing of all-Black schools and the fact that White parents did not want their children taught by Black teachers.[26] *Brown* promised educational opportunity, social mobility, and higher graduation rates. Six decades later, researchers have found that students of color make up a majority of public school enrollment, while White students make up more than half of the nation's overall enrollment; most White students attend a school where three-quarters of their peers are White too. Currently, less than 2 percent of teachers are Black men; White men and women make up more than 80 percent of the teaching force.[27] Teacher retention is also at an all-time low.[28] Many White teachers are by-products of White flight and White rage. They have grown up living and learning in communities created by their grandparents' or great-grandparents' hate and fear of darkness. Many of these teachers are unaware of how their lily-White communities were established in and have upheld Whiteness. This lack of awareness, of course, often leads them to measure their communities against the urban school communities they teach in, which makes subscribing to stereotypes easier.

For example, some of the most hypersegregated schools are concentrated in the urban centers of Chicago, New York, Detroit, Boston, St. Louis, and Pittsburgh. In metro Los Angeles, 30 percent of Latinx students attend a school where Whites make up 1 percent or less of the enrollment.[29] Nationwide, 80 percent of Latinx students and 74 percent of Black students attend majority non-White schools. America's schools are also segregated based on class. On the sixtieth anniversary of *Brown*, the federal Government Accountability Office released a predictable report, if you understand White rage, stating that "high-poverty, high-minority schools are under-resourced and over-disciplined."[30] Schools located in low-income neighborhoods are underfunded, which means they have fewer school resources, less school personnel, and, ultimately, less social and economic mobility. Black students are six times more likely than White students to attend a high-poverty school. Latinx students face triple segregation: by race, poverty, and language. Overall, only 9 percent of low-income students graduate from college.[31] Given the hypersegregation of today's schools and the lack of economic and social mobility for dark students, it is safe to say that *Brown's* mission has failed.

The latest iteration of the educational survival complex is the charter school movement. Like most liberal egalitarian efforts, charter schools perpetuate inequalities, pulling high-achieving students from traditional public schools. Many charter schools are operated by education management organizations (EMOs) that work to privatize public education, indirectly and directly. Moreover, successful charter schools push low-income dark families out of their own neighborhoods. Gentrification is displacing millions of such families. Atlanta, where I live, is gentrifying at twice the rate of other American cities such as Washington, DC, New Orleans, Portland, and Seattle. I have watched traditionally Black neighborhoods become overwhelmingly White in a matter of years. In 2014, Atlanta's inequality gap was the highest in the nation, and by 2016 it was still third.[32] Atlanta's Black neighborhoods like the Old Fourth Ward—where Dr. Martin Luther King Jr. grew up, a prominent Black community sixty years ago—are almost half White, with rising home prices pushing dark folx to the edges of the city and society. A high-performing school, whether charter or traditional, will expedite the displacement of dark families.

I would be remiss if I did not mention the "no excuses" teaching approach of many charter schools around the country. Charter school networks such as Success Academy and KIPP popularized aggressive, paternalistic, and racist ideological teaching practices on dark bodies. The boards of directors operating these charter schools are typically composed of wealthy philanthropists, corporate foundations, and Wall Street hedge fund managers who believe dark children need discipline, character education, rudimentary academic skills, and full submission to White economic demands.[33] In his book *Work Hard, Be Hard: Journeys Through "No Excuses" Teaching,* Jim Horn documents in great detail the unrelenting pressure on students to meet education benchmarks—what some KIPP school officials called the "plan of attack"—and the resulting suffering that dark families experience at charter schools. For example, when a group of fourth-grade students failed to use test-taking strategies, the leader at the school sent this email to fourth-grade teachers:

> We can NOT let up on them. . . . Any scholar who is not using the plan of attack will go to effort academy, have their parent called, and will miss electives. This is serious business, and there has to be misery felt for kids who are not doing what is expected of them.[34]

Dark children at KIPP cannot fail, cannot express their stress, cannot feel pain from a world that rejects them, and cannot make mistakes, one of the critical and necessary experiences of childhood. The "no excuses" model is just another form of zero tolerance. These schools function to feed the school-to-prison pipeline that targets dark children. In March 2016, the Civil Rights Project at UCLA released data from one of the largest studies ever to research school discipline records, involving more than 5,250 charter schools.[35] The study found that charter schools suspend Black students and students with disabilities at highly disproportionate rates compared with White and non-disabled students. For example, the study reported that five hundred charter schools suspended Black students at a rate of 10 percentage points higher than their White peers. This has a direct impact on children's futures, as extensive research demonstrates that high suspension rates are part of the school-to-prison pipeline. Again, it's another way in which the educational survival complex and the prison-industrial complex are tied together to profit from dark suffering.

In 2015, officials at Brooklyn's Success Academy Fort Greene were publicly shamed for maintaining a "Got to Go" list of students who were blacklisted from the school's network because of repeated suspensions and/or their parents not complying with school rules. Charter school networks like Success Academy are notorious for "coaching" students and their families out of school. In 2017, parents sued KIPP Houston for charging students for reading materials and classroom supplies. KIPP is a free public charter that receives state and local funds to pay for school supplies and books, like any other public school, but is also well-supported nationally by corporate and private donors. An investigation found that KIPP's Houston branch collected approximately $2.3 million in student fees from low-income families during the 2015–2016 school year.[36] These families are now demanding their money back.

After all the dark suffering in and outside of school, students of charter schools who are not pushed out—particularly at those schools that serve dark, low-income communities—do not graduate from college at dramatically higher rates than the same demographic of students who attend traditional public schools. According to the Equality of Opportunity Project at Harvard University, the American dream, if there ever was one for dark people, is fading fast. Children have a 50 percent chance of earning more or the same as their parents. A half century ago, that possibility was 90 percent. Even a person's life expectancy is tied to his or her education, income, and location. Data suggest that "for the poorest Americans, life expectancies are 6 years higher in New York than in Detroit."[37]

Profiting from dark children's suffering is not just for the testing, prison, and textbook industries but also for private investors and hedge funds. In 2016, a group of education researchers sounded the alarm comparing charter schools to subprime mortgages.[38] Subprime mortgages are high-risk mortgage loans that were common leading up to the 2007–2008 financial crisis. Banks specifically targeted Black people by issuing loans they knew they could not repay by imposing unfair and aggressive loan terms, a practice called predatory lending. This practice is one of the many reasons the housing bubble burst. Also, a high number of Black people were deceived into taking out home loans that ruined their chances of ever building wealth. Similarly, researchers point out that there is a charter school bubble growing too.

One investment strategy used by corporate school reformers (akin to disaster capitalists) is the Community Renewal Tax Relief Act of 2000, which provides tax incentives for seven years to businesses that reside and hire residents in economically depressed communities. To increase profits, investors lobby federal and local governments to ease regulations and restrictions that limit the number of charter schools in a particular state or school district. Deregulating charter school growth allows corporate school reformers to open up public schools to the highest bidder. This scheme motivates investors such as Facebook CEO Mark Zuckerberg to donate half a million dollars of stock to organizations that distribute charter school funding.[39] Zuckerberg also opened his own foundation, Startup:Education, to build more charter schools.[40] The real estate industry receives massive tax cuts for buying inner-city schools, homes, and buildings. Many of the most über-rich hedge fund operators have close ties to charter schools. David Tepper ($3.5 billion in earnings in 2013) founded Appaloosa Management and Better Education for Kids; Steven A. Cohen ($2.4 billion in 2013) of SAC Capital Advisors donated $10 million to the Achievement First charter school network.[41]

The push to open so many charter schools, when only 17 percent of them academically outperform public schools, is tied to profiting from dark suffering. Corporate school reformers prey on the suffering and hopes of dark communities, and just like the subprime-mortgages practice of predatory lending, they lack regulation and oversight. Once the charter school bubble bursts, dark communities will be left with what education researcher Gloria Ladson-Billings calls "education debt."[42] According to Ladson-Billings, education debt has accumulated over time, composed of the US' historical, economic, sociopolitical, and moral debts.[43] Corporate school reformers profit from the history of oppression of dark people. Their earnings rely on the stability of dark children and their families surviving while preying on their desire to do more than just survive. They make money on dark families' dreams of thriving through education.

All of this reform implemented by the educational survival complex has made billions for the testing industry, the hedge fund industry, the textbook industry, the housing industry, and elitist nonprofit organizations that perpetuate and operate from a stereotypical master narrative regarding dark children and their families but, without fail, leave dark families struggling to survive. Corporate school reformers are superpredators too. But what about the spirit enduring in constant survival mode, which is violence by another name? This type of violence is less visceral and seemingly less tragic than the physical acts of murder at the hands of White mobs or White men acting on their White rage, but the racist, hateful language and systemic, institutionalized, antidark, state-sanctioned violence that dark children endure on a daily basis in the educational survival complex murders the spirit; it's a slow death, but a death nonetheless.

SPIRIT-MURDERING

In October 2015, a Black girl at Spring Valley High School in Columbia, South Carolina, was thrown from her desk and across the floor by the school's resource officer, Ben Fields. According to reports, Fields was called when the student refused to hand over her cell phone to her teacher. The incident was recorded by two classmates in the room. To add insult to injury, when another Black female student spoke out about the incident, she was arrested for "disturbing the school." Little is known about the young Black girl who was body-slammed by her school's resource officer; however, we know she was recently placed in foster care after the death of her mother. After the assault, reports did surface that the students of Spring Valley referred to Fields as "the Incredible Hulk" because of his violent behavior with students at the school.

Six months before the Spring Valley High School incident in South Carolina, a Georgia principal verbally assaulted the students and families of TNT Academy, an alternative high school, at the school's graduation ceremony. After the school's principal, Nancy Gordeuk, erroneously dismissed the graduating class before the school's valedictorian gave his speech, she asked the crowd to return to hear his remarks. When it seemed that attendees were not following Gordeuk's instructions, she snidely remarked to a predominantly Black audience, "Look who's leaving—all the Black people." Not unexpectedly, students and their families were offended by her racist statement, and the crowd exploded in protest.

In 2016, Ryan Turk, a Black middle school student in Prince William County, Virginia, took a sixty-five-cent milk carton from the school's cafeteria. Ryan admitted he cut the lunch line and proceeded to take a carton of milk without going through the line. The school's resource officer witnessed the incident, then took Ryan to the principal's office, where his mother says he was searched for drugs. According to police, Ryan became hostile and was placed in handcuffs. Ultimately, Ryan was charged with disorderly conduct and petit larceny. Ryan is allowed free milk as part of the school's free- and reduced-price-lunch program. Instead of having a conversation with Ryan about following procedures, police arrested him. Ryan turned down a plea of nonjudicial punishment because he felt that he did not steal the carton of milk since he received free lunch, raising the question: how can you steal something that is rightfully yours? The prosecutor dropped the charges before the case went to trial.

In 2013, Vanessa VanDyke, a Black twelve-year-old student in Orlando, was threatened with expulsion from her private Christian school for not cutting her natural hair because school officials characterized her hair as a "distraction." Vanessa was being teased and bullied about her beautiful Afro. Vanessa told local reporters, "I'm depressed about leaving my friends and people that I've known for a while, but I'd rather have that than the principals and administrators picking on me and saying that I should change my hair."[44] Facing public pressure and outrage, Vanessa's school withdrew the threat of expulsion. That same year, in Tulsa, Oklahoma, a seven-year-old Black girl, Tiana Parker, was sent home from school for having locked hair. The school's official policy stated, "Hairstyles such as dreadlocks, afros, mohawks, and other faddish styles are unacceptable." This policy is not just about hair; the policy is informed by racist ideas of Black peoples' unfitness, unattractiveness, and inferiority.

In June 2016, Kim Stidham, a charter school principal in Duval County, Florida, posted on Facebook a song with the lyrics, "Take all of the rope in Texas, find a tall oak tree, round up all them bad boys, hang them high in the street for all the people to see."[45] Stidham released a statement after she came under fire for her post:

> I am absolutely devastated that my personal political views were perceived to be racist in any way. I am a firm believer in equality,

justice and respect for all individuals and I recognize now that some of my posts could have been misunderstood. I appreciate the fact that those who were offended brought this to my attention so that I could rectify the situation. I encourage anyone who has any concerns about this to come to me directly so that we can discuss it further.[46]

Her statement is a perfect example of how racist educators believe their actions outside the class in no way impact their classroom or school. She is "devastated" that her personal views could be seen as racist, but history confirms her racism. Black women, men, and children were rounded up and killed by White mobs; there is no other way to "perceive" her words. Also, people who are "firm believer[s] in equality, justice and respect" can be racist; merely saying the words does not make you a freedom fighter—your actions do. Lastly, Stidham did not apologize because in her mind she did nothing wrong. Racist educators seldom take responsibility for their racist actions and believe the resulting situation is just a misunderstanding or a lack of cultural awareness; again, this denies dark people's knowledge of how racism works, and we should know.

To be clear, all of these racist, antidark, emotionally and physically violent school incidents happened before the election of Donald Trump. After the election of 2016, *Mother Jones* published an article titled "Bullying in Schools Is Out of Control Since Election Day."[47] The article documented cases of anti-Black, anti-Muslim, and anti-Semitic incidents that were normalizing everyday racial aggression in classrooms and on college campuses across the country. The day after the election, at DeWitt Junior High School in Michigan, a group of boys formed a wall, using their bodies, to block a fellow student, Maliah Gonzalez, from her locker. As they blocked her, they chanted, "Donald Trump for president. Let's build the wall. Let's make America great again. You need to go back to Mexico."[48] In York, Pennsylvania, a video was reported that showed two students carrying a Donald Trump/Mike Pence sign and shouting, "White power" in the hallways of York Country School of Technology.[49] At

Council Rock High School North in Newtown, Pennsylvania, someone wrote, "I Love Trump," drew swastikas, and added homophobic language on a piece of paper found in the girls' bathroom.[50] At the same school, another student in the girls' bathroom found a note stating, "If Trump wins, watch out!"[51] A Latinx student also uncovered a note in her backpack telling her to return to Mexico.

In the summer of 2017, Nicholas Dean, principal of the Crescent Leadership Academy in New Orleans, was fired for wearing rings associated with White nationalism and the Nazi movement. The Southern Poverty Law Center stated that Dean's entire outfit, not just the rings, was the attire of someone in the alt-right. Crescent Leadership Academy's student body is predominantly Black. In Albuquerque, New Mexico, two high school students Photoshopped a picture showing two Black students surrounded by White students wearing KKK hoods. In Ohio, a teacher was caught dragging a little Black girl down the hallway by her arm like a hunter after killing her prey. In Baton Rouge, Louisiana, a principal was arrested for felony cruelty to a juvenile for locking a five-year-old girl in a closet at school. In 2018, a third-grade teacher in Scottsdale, Arizona, Bonnie Godin Verne, suggested that killing immigrants is a better option than deporting them. In New York City's Bronx borough, Patricia Cummings, while teaching a lesson about slavery, put her foot on a Black student's back and asked the student, "See how it feels to be a slave?"[52]

I must also mention the alt-right rally that took place in Charlottesville, Virginia, in August 2017. These emboldened White supremacists, who take their lead from President Trump, shouted their racist and hateful rallying cries of "You will not replace us" and "Jews will not replace us" while surrounding a statue of Thomas Jefferson (who owned slaves) and condemning the removal of a statue of Robert E. Lee, a Confederate general, in Charlottesville. A thirty-two-year-old White woman, Heather Heyer, who was there to counterprotest White nationalists, was killed at the protest when James Alex Fields, a White supremacist, drove his car into the group of protesters who were standing up for justice. Trump refused to condemn these White supremacists and their action, and days following

Heyer's death, Trump called the White supremacists who invaded Charlottesville "some very fine people."

In the spring of 2018, school officials in Citrus County School District in Florida learned that one of their social studies teachers, Dayanna Volitich, was the host of a White nationalist podcast called *Unapologetic*. Volitich used the pseudonym Tiana Dalichov on her show. On her podcast she declared that science has proven that certain races are smarter, bragged about teaching White nationalism in her classroom, suggested that Muslims be eradicated from the earth, pitched anti-Semitic conspiracy theories, and, of course, denounced White privilege as not being real. School officials removed Volitich from the classroom; however, she was not fired immediately. I guess they needed time to determine just how racist she was outside and inside of school. In the summer of 2018, Geye Hamby, superintendent of Buford City Schools in Georgia, was caught on tape talking about killing "niggers." He was put on leave by the district. This atmosphere is no way to live or learn. School districts' spokespersons and President Trump portray these incidents as isolated events, the work of a few overzealous, culturally insensitive but "good" teachers, students, and community members. Mainstream society uses the "few bad apples" argument, which misdiagnoses the "systemic and ideological production of race itself which is squarely centered in White supremacy."[53] These school attacks are more than just racist acts by misguided school officials, youth, and community members; put into a historical context, these attacks "draw, secure, police, and legitimize the parameters of Whiteness and non-Whiteness."[54]

These school attacks also spirit-murder dark children. Legal scholar Patricia Williams argued that racism is more than just physical pain; racism robs dark people of their humanity and dignity and leaves personal, psychological, and spiritual injuries.[55] Racism literally murders your spirit. Racism is traumatic because it is a loss of protection, safety, nurturance, and acceptance—all things children need to be educated.[56] The White rage in our schools murders dark students' spirits. Physical survival is not enough. Spirit-murder is not only about race and racism; dark people's other identity categories, such as gender, citizenship, religion, language, class, ethnicity, nationality, and queerness, are additional, distinct factors driving discrimination, bigotry, and violence.[57] This state of affairs underlines the importance of intersectionality: "Ordinary people can draw upon intersectionality as an analytic tool when they recognize that they need better frameworks to grapple with complex discrimination that they face."[58] We must use all the analytic tools available to understand how our children are spirit-murdered and educated in a state of perpetual survival mode for the benefit of the educational survival complex.

LIFE

What I am describing is a life of exhaustion, a life of doubt, a life of state-sanctioned violence, and a life consumed with the objective of *surviving*. Survival is existing and being educated in an antidark world, which is not living or learning at all. It is trying to survive in, and at the same time understand and make sense of, a world and its schools that are reliant on dark disposability and the narratives necessary to bring about that disposability. This existence is not truly living nor is it a life of mattering. As dark people, we are trying to survive the conditions that make the dark body, mind, and spirit breakable and disposable.

The racist ideas that condition all of us and take hold of so many, according to Ibram X. Kendi, author of *Stamped from the Beginning: The Definitive History of Racist Ideas in America*, are not the work of ignorant and hateful people: "Time and again, powerful and brilliant men and women have produced racist ideas in order to justify the racist policies of their era, in order to redirect the blame for their era's racial disparities away from those policies and onto Black people." Kendi's words are an introduction to understanding that America's deep entrenchment in racist ideas that produce discriminatory policies, which engineered "mass incarceration, beatings, and the killings of Black people by law enforcement," is the same reality that functions as a site of dispensability for dark people in America's schools.[59]

Living under the surveillance of a superpredator is a slow death of the body, mind, and spirit—if the system does not speed up your expiration date.

Schools are mirrors of our society; educational justice cannot and will not happen in a vacuum or with pedagogies that undergird the educational survival complex. We need pedagogies that support social movements. I hear teachers say all the time, "I close my classroom door and teach." This strategy helps teachers survive the disempowering and stressful environment, irrelevant curriculums, and bureaucratic mess of education, but it does not change the field or the context in which youth are being disposed of; it may just prolong the inevitable. Ta-Nehisi Coates writes,

> The streets were not my only problem. If the streets shackled my right leg, the schools shackled my left. Fail to comprehend the streets and you gave up your body now. But fail to comprehend the schools and you gave up your body later. Suffered at the hands of both, but I resent the schools more. . . . The world had no time for the childhoods of Black boys and girls. . . . When our elders presented school to us, they did not present it as a place of high learning but as a means of escape from death and penal warehousing. . . . Schools did not reveal truths, they concealed them. Perhaps they must be burned away so that the heart of this thing might be known.[60]

At the heart of this thing are racism, persisting segregation, and violence. Dark people within America are the disposable class of people, inside and outside the classroom. As educators, we must accept that schools are spaces of Whiteness, White rage, and disempowerment. We cannot fall into narratives of racial progress that romanticize "how far we've come" or suggest that success comes from darks being more like Whites. Jean Anyon reminds us, "As a nation, we have been counting on education to solve the problems of unemployment, joblessness, and poverty for many years. But education did not cause these problems, and education cannot solve them."[61] Education is not the antecedent of failing schools, poverty, homelessness, police brutality, and/or crime. Racism is; racism that is built on centuries of ideas that seek to confuse and manipulate we who are dark into never mattering to one another or this country.

CHAPTER 3

MATTERING

*When you know your name, you should hang on to it, for un-
less it is noted down and remembered, it will die when you do.*

—TONI MORRISON[1]

*It's a system of power that is always deciding in the name of
humanity who deserves to be remembered and who deserves
to be forgotten. . . . We are much more than we are told. We
are much more beautiful.*

—EDUARDO GALEANO[2]

GIVE THEM *HELL*

As a kid, I did not take school seriously. I liked my teachers and
my classmates, but I never felt a connection to the school beyond
my mother, Patty, telling me I had to go. I took her instructions to
heart. My mother and father were hardworking Black folx, and they
required the same of their kids. They went to work every day, and so
did we: school was our job. Then, at the age of sixteen, my siblings
and I, in addition to attending school, had to get jobs, a requirement
for living in Patty's house. With that level of independence came the
responsibility of paying our own bills for school supplies and clothes,
especially sneakers (like my $150 Jordans). Though my parents were
far from perfect, they instilled in their children the values of hard
work and education. Reflecting on that dynamic as an adult, I realize
the reasons for their insistence.

My parents wholeheartedly trusted my teachers with my education; they had no choice. My father had an eighth-grade education, and my mother earned her GED. They believed education was the great equalizer, but there was a caveat: education was not to be confused with common sense in the Love house. Education was what you learned in school and common sense was what you learned to survive, and they taught us that upward mobility done with your dignity intact depended on a combination of the two. Common sense meant trusting your gut, reading between the lines, listening before speaking, and never, I mean never, telling your family's business, especially to White folx.

We never explicitly discussed racism because it needed no exploration; racism was simply an ever-present part of our lives, like oxygen—but unlike racism, oxygen is necessary to survive. It was implicitly understood in our house that you had to be twice as smart as White folx, had to never let down your guard, never lower your head in defeat, and had to possess a confidence that should never be mistaken for arrogance. To my parents, if you were going to be something in this world, being an A student was just the tip of the iceberg.

Before I left for school in the morning, especially if I had a big basketball game, my mother always said, "Give them *hell*." Of course, "them" referred to anyone standing in the way of the basketball hoop or my dreams. She still gives me that advice to this day. Though not an activist or a community organizer, my mother, a retired school lunch lady, practices a politics of refusal, whether or not she identifies it as such. She says she is just blunt and forthright, and does not let anyone stop her from getting where she has to go in the world. Still, her particular brand of politics of refusal was instilled in me as a young child. A politics of refusal is one of the necessary components of activism vital to dark folx' survival and is fundamental to abolitionist teaching. Patty experienced racism growing up in Rochester, New York. She and her nine brothers and sisters lived through the 1964 Rochester riots, sparked by police brutality, which spanned three days, killing four people and injuring 350.

She attended school during the early years of desegregation. Her stories of growing up as a Black girl in Rochester are stories of struggle, perseverance, and learning how to survive to make the world not better for her children but a bit easier. She survived because her mother was a master of the politics of refusal. My grandmother was from South Carolina. She moved to upstate New York for the same reasons many Black folx moved from the South: jobs and the hope of less racial violence. Thus, these two women are my survival blueprints. They taught me to stand up for myself because it was the one thing Whiteness could not take, and maybe the one thing that would postpone the inevitable: the obstruction of my dreams because I was a little Black girl.

Therefore, I learned above all else to protect my dignity. My dignity was never to be compromised, which meant never compromising my voice and my connection to how I mattered in this world. When you compromise your voice, you compromise your dignity. No dignity, no power. Knowing I had a voice backed by common sense, which I understood was supposed to be used to protect myself, was one of the most powerful things I have ever been taught. To my mother, common sense was everything; that's where you speak from and then education follows. When I called my mother to inform her that I wanted to go back to school to pursue a PhD, she simply told me, "*Don't be an educated fool.*" That was it, but I knew exactly what she meant: earning a PhD would mean nothing to my mother if I forgot where I came from and how to relate to the people who protected my dreams and my education. What good is an education if you must shed who you are? Authenticity was a fundamental component to "giving them *hell.*" My mother desperately wanted her children to be themselves. I never once had a conversation with my mother about my sexuality. We both knew I was a lesbian, so there was really nothing else to discuss. To be honest, Patty knew before me.

That said, my siblings and I would be in deep trouble if we tried to pretend to be something we were not. My mother did not like people who changed their voices around White folx to sound more proper or

Black folx who put other Black folx down in front of Whites folx. She taught us to take pride in who we were: working-class Black kids from upstate New York who always walked into a room with their heads held high. So, with that upbringing, I went to elementary school a confident, skinny little girl without one shy bone in my body. I was Patty and Honey Love's daughter, but, unfortunately, that was not enough.

IRRELEVANCY

From kindergarten to third grade, I attended a diverse Catholic school in the heart of Rochester. By diverse, in upstate New York, I mean Black and White kids went to school together. The school was predominantly Black; however, about 20 percent of the students were White. Inside the walls of the school, students were loved. The teachers were kind, tolerant, and compassionate but focused mainly on academic rigor. I liked going there, but I did not understand why school was so important. There was no connection to my history or my community, nor any discussion to explain why drugs, guns, and violence were becoming everyday problems in my city. I did not have the language or understanding to express it, but I knew the city was changing. Working-class Black families—families I knew—were falling apart due to the disappearance of manufacturing jobs, the stresses of financial instability, and the Reagan administration's "War on Drugs." In what felt like the blink of an eye, dark kids, like myself, were labeled criminals; First Lady Nancy Reagan was on TV telling us to "Just Say No," and we were all given DARE (Drug Abuse Resistance Education) shirts as Officer Friendly reminded us not to become another statistic.

The racial divide in the city was high, and the last few White folx who could afford to leave the city did. Dark children were deemed lazy, unruly, promiscuous, and violent. Our humanity rested in White America's racist imagination, which always turns to antidark policy. Take, for example, *The Negro Family: The Case for National Action*, also called the Moynihan Report, released in 1965, a year after the Rochester riots, by President Lyndon B. Johnson's administration. It argued that discrimination forced Black families into "a matriarchal structure" that "seriously retards the progress of the group as a whole, and imposes a crushing burden on the Negro, and in consequence, on a great many Negro women."[3] The Moynihan Report—which was leaked—claimed that Black men's feelings of alienation led to high rates of poverty and child abuse and to low educational outcomes. In short, Moynihan branded and blamed the Black family structure for Black folx' inability and unwillingness to assimilate into White American culture.

When uprisings occurred and dark folx took to the streets in protest, according to the Moynihan Report, "rioters" suffered from schizophrenia, which was labeled a "Black disease." Rioters embodied what racist criminologist Marvin Wolfgang called, in reference to urban Blacks folx, a "subculture of violence."[4] Moynihan's views became widespread and dominated the narrative explaining dark life to White folx (and to some dark folx too). To be clear, conservative think tanks such as the Heritage Foundation, the Hoover Institution, and the Manhattan Institute still celebrate the report and used aspects of it to explain the uprisings after the killing of eighteen-year-old Michael Brown in Ferguson, Missouri, in 2014.[5]

Moynihan, a Democrat, wrote the 1965 report in his role as assistant secretary of labor under President Johnson. Four years after the report's publication, Moynihan was named President Richard Nixon's urban affairs adviser. Nixon named himself the law and order president; he believed that Blacks and Puerto Ricans, especially those with their fists in the air shouting Black and Brown Power, were the reason the country lacked law and order. Nixon's racist, combative, state-sanctioned, violent tactics killed and criminalized dark folx in order to appeal to White voters.

Back in Rochester, I was living under the conditions of a "human hierarchy," unaware of the history that produced this feeling of irrelevancy. I knew my family loved me, that my dreams mattered to them, that my voice had power, but I could not see myself as the world saw me. Tucked away inside St. Monica's, teachers either did not know the conditions of "human hierarchy" or saw themselves as liberators with their anti-Black, color-blind rhetoric. As a result, I was a lost kid. I needed more than love and compassion; I needed to know what folx who looked like me meant to the world beyond what Officer Friendly thought of my friends and me.

In a series of unfortunate events, I left St. Monica's at the end of third grade. My parents fell behind in tuition, I was steadily falling behind academically, and I was mad at the world for letting me down. School did not come easily to me; it never has. I needed more time; I needed school to slow down. From the outset, I remember wishing my teachers and my classmates would just come to a screeching halt so I could catch up. My voice, the voice needed for survival, could not be heard from so far behind. My most important tools—my opinions, my ideas of right and wrong—were in a holding cell. I could not find a space where I mattered. I was an average student—sometimes below average. I do not remember winning any awards or thinking deeply about anything. I entered school every day because I had to.

My teachers were concerned; they did not understand how a child from a two-parent home, with a brother and sister who had been exceptional students, could be so disengaged. My mother was furious at my teachers for letting me fall behind and waiting until the end of third grade to inform her. By the time my mother was done giving those teachers hell, we needed to leave St. Monica's, and the teachers were happy to see us go.

With a Jheri curl and legs as long and skinny as telephone poles, I started fourth grade at School #19, a public school. A Black school. The students and most of the teachers were Black. There, I was introduced to my first Black teacher, Mrs. Johnson. I had never seen a woman, regardless of race, so powerful, so commanding, and so stern. She was also tall and skinny, like me, and wore braces, which I needed. Most intriguing of all, Mrs. Johnson was from the South— New Orleans, to be exact. Mrs. Johnson did not just love her students, she fundamentally believed that we mattered. She made us believe that our lives were entangled with hers and that caring for us meant caring for herself. Not to mention, parents feared Mrs. Johnson, even my mother. I distinctly remember walking into class, looking up at Mrs. Johnson, and realizing my class-clown days were over. I was relieved. I was ready to get my voice back. I was not scared of Mrs. Johnson; I wanted her to think I was smart, funny, and kind, characteristics I knew she valued.

Mrs. Johnson had beautiful penmanship; she wore colorful dresses to school and demanded excellence. She was also keenly aware that school had to matter to us beyond our grades; we needed a survival plan. Mrs. Johnson taught as if the fate of her and her children was tied to ours. She shared stories with her students of her childhood in New Orleans. She was vulnerable in front of the class. She called home to speak to your parents about you as a person, not just a student. She had a sense of responsibility for her students, and we were a family. You did not want to disappoint Mrs. Johnson because then you disappointed the class and your family. It was a collective spirit of accountability, love, and purpose. She genuinely listened to us, took up our concerns in her teaching, and made sure each voice in the classroom was heard. After I had been in her class for a few weeks she knew I was behind and that my home life was unraveling. At the time, my mother and father were hooked on drugs and my siblings were off living their adult lives. I am not sure how Mrs. Johnson knew, but she did. She never looked down on me or lowered her expectations of me. If anything, she demanded more, with a keen understanding of my life and what was in front of me.

Of course, Mrs. Johnson could not work a miracle and bring me to grade level in one year, but she gave me purpose, and I grew as a person. Mrs. Johnson allowed me to see why I mattered to myself, and another local program, FIST (Fighting Ignorance and Spending Truth), politicized me. Without these two imperative elements (mattering and becoming politicized), I would not have survived school and the larger systems of the world. Those of us who make it through school leave with skills and scars that are necessary for survival in this racist, sexist, and capitalistic world. The scars of systemic oppression are real and traumatic. Sadly, in that way, school is a battlefield. For many dark children, if you cannot survive school, it will be almost impossible to survive outside its walls.

FIST

During my year with Mrs. Johnson, I also participated in a program run by a local college student, Thabiti Bruce Boone, focused on youth empowerment and activism for neighborhood kids ages ten to sixteen: FIST. It was my first experience with a male teacher, a Black male teacher. Thabiti, a young single dad, was a great basketball player and loved hip-hop. He had something in common with every kid in the room. On Saturday mornings and some weekdays, we would gather and Thabiti would introduce the work and ideas of Angela Davis, the Black Panthers, Black Liberation, Malcolm X, Nelson Mandela, and leaders of our own community. At the time, I did not think of the program as civics education or ideas of mattering; I just knew it felt freeing, empowering, and secretive. Even in Mrs. Johnson's class we did not learn about Black people who resisted oppression outside of Dr. Martin Luther King Jr. and Rosa Parks. Their stories were diluted of any ideas of Black Power. King, Parks, Malcolm, and the Black Panthers all believed in empowerment, self-determination, unity, and cultural pride. King, when speaking at the Southern Christian Leadership Conference, told the crowd that the Negro must "say to himself and to the world . . . I'm Black, but I'm Black and beautiful." Being in FIST help me find meaning and purpose as a Black kid.

In FIST we learned that being Black was beautiful, to love our skin, that our darkness had a history of resistance, pride, community, joy, love, and understanding, and that we mattered to our community, to the world, and to ourselves. We also learned that Black power meant grassroots organizing, human rights, and cooperative economic strategies. The basis of our work was self-determination. We saw ourselves taking up physical, intellectual, political, and creative space in places we had thought were unimaginable. We walked around with our little fists held proudly in the air, feeling powerful, in love with ourselves and one another, giving them *hell*, civically engaged, and unified.

LOVING BLACKNESS

The writer bell hooks argues that loving Blackness is an act of political resistance because we all have internalized racism, regardless of the color of our skin, which operates to devalue Blackness, but she argues that Black people need to love themselves not in spite of their Blackness but because of their Blackness.[6] I learned to truly love myself as a member of FIST. Loving my Blackness was the first step in my politicization, mattering, and wanting to thrive.

I kept my membership in FIST a secret from my teachers at school because it felt different from anything I had experienced at St. Monica's or #19. My parents knew I was in FIST; however, they did not know the extent of what I was learning. I was afraid another adult would take my newfound power away. My mother wanted me to use my voice but she was old school; a child stays in a child's place, and we were doing grown-up business (one of the many contradictions of her parenting). So, I found my voice by using my mother's advice, grounded in a history that, intentional or not, was kept from me. Through FIST, I was beginning to understand the ways in which school did and did not matter while also learning how I mattered.

In *Teaching to Transgress: Education as the Practice of Freedom*, hooks walks the reader through how her schooling experiences changed after desegregation. Before her school was integrated—I would say colonized—teachers understood that their job of teaching Black children was a political act rooted in antiracist struggle. She writes that she experienced her all-Black grade school as a space of "learning as revolution."[7] After her school was colonized, she writes,

> School changed utterly with racial integration. Gone was the messianic zeal to transform our minds and beings that had characterized teachers and their pedagogical practices in our all-Black schools. Knowledge was suddenly about information. It had no

relation to how one lived, behaved. It was no longer connected to antiracist struggle. . . . When we entered racist, desegregated, White school we left a world where teachers believed that to educate Black children rightly would require a political commitment.[8]

The kind of schooling hooks experienced once her school was filled with White teachers is the only experience I knew until third grade. I have taught so many future educators and worked with hundreds of in-service teachers who profess to love all kids and have good intentions to be fair and just in their classrooms, yet they write, say, and partake in racist actions and posts online about dark children loosely masked in the language of low expectations, of judging low-income parents and dark children's behavior. Furthermore, there are so many White liberal teachers who think racism is something singular to the far right. Racism is not exclusive to one political party or a particular type of White person. White, well-meaning, liberal teachers can be racist too. Therefore, understanding how racism works and understanding how White privilege functions within our society does not bring us any closer to justice, and it certainly does not undo the educational survival complex. Knowing these truths is the first step to justice, but it's only a start.

Too often we think the work of fighting oppression is just intellectual. The real work is personal, emotional, spiritual, and communal. It is explicit, with a deep and intense understanding that loving Blackness is an act of political resistance, and therefore it is the fundamental aspect to teaching dark kids. I do not mean just to teach dark children their ABCs and 123s; I mean to teach them to demand what Anna Julia Cooper called "undisputed dignity." To call for "recognition of one's inherent humanity" with the courage, persistence, vigilance, and the visionary imagination of an abolitionist.[9]

For those reasons, the work must be straightforward. FIST and Thabiti were explicit, and explicit was exactly what I needed. In FIST there was no questioning why we were there and what the objective was: we were being politicized through antiracist struggle with a global perspective, specifically emphasizing our own communities. Attending school Monday through Friday and FIST on weekends for three years, I was able to draw a sharp distinction between the two. School talked a good game, but my teachers' actions spoke louder than their words, even in Mrs. Johnson's class. I had to learn despite school, not because of it. School mattered because it provided the testing ground in which I learned ways to resist and navigate racism, the low expectations, the stereotypes, the spirit-murdering, all the forms of dark suffering, gender suffering, queer suffering, religious suffering, and class suffering. I learned that to succeed at school—by "succeed" I do not mean getting good grades but leaving every day with my darkness intact or only slightly bruised—I had to practice a politics of refusal, love my Blackness as an act of political resistance, and give them hell. FIST provided the fuel and roadmap to survive school unbroken. It added bass to my voice so I could critique, provoke, and resist. FIST taught me that if I could survive school, I had a better chance of surviving the world.

In FIST we felt like leaders because the structure of the organization was dependent on youth leadership in the board of directors, committee members, and the staff. We learned to understand our community needs by studying our community and studying the philosophies of freedom fighters who resisted oppression. Too often in schools we learn and teach about oppression and injustice, but rarely are we taught or do we teach how ordinary people fought for justice. In schools, we occasionally learn that injustice is met with resistance; we do not learn that dark folx have always practiced a politics of refusal that looks different depending on the person or the community. Today we hardly ever teach that dark people fought to matter, wishing one day to thrive and taking calculated steps to benefit the next generation.

The year after Mrs. Johnson's class, I was in Mr. Clayton's class Monday through Friday. On the weekends, I learned what I would need as a dark person to thrive beyond the walls of my school. School was for my survival; FIST taught me to thrive as a dark child. Both of these learning experiences were equally important to me. Mr. Clayton wore a tie and slacks every day to school. He was my first and only Black male teacher in a formal school setting until college. Like Mrs. Johnson, he never wore sneakers or dressed down. He called all his students by their last names with a Mr. or Miss inserted in the front.

Around that time, I started coming to class dirty after playing basketball with some of the boys before school started. My parents left for work in the mornings so it was my responsibility to get to school on time. I would play basketball in the rain and snow; I did not care, I just wanted to play. One morning I came in looking a mess. Mr. Clayton called me, Miss Love, over to his desk. I felt so important. As I smiled at him, he said, "Miss Love, you are pretty good." At the time, those words from my Black male teacher were all the validation I needed to keep playing. But Mr. Clayton never let my love for basketball stop my development as a young woman. He told me that he knew I played basketball before school every day and that he did not want me to stop, but I could not continue to come to his class filthy. I remember him saying it from such a place of love and real concern. He told me to start ironing a change of clothes in the morning to bring to school. He also told me that he knew something was going on at home and that I could talk to him. I never did. Reflecting on it now, I wish I had. But being young and juggling so many emotions, I simply was not able to do so.

Mr. Clayton and Mrs. Johnson were my teacher twins: they both were tall, skinny, and demanded respect. To me, they were both more than teachers or role models; they were necessary parental figures. Of course, I needed my own parents, too, but I required a village to survive and understand how I mattered in this world. My parents could not do it all. Dark children cannot thrive without a community of love, refusal, protection, knowledge, and resource-sharing. Mrs. Johnson, Mr. Clayton, and Thabiti knew all too well this reality for their students.

A recent study examining the school records of more than one hundred thousand Black elementary students in North Carolina found that having just one Black teacher in third, fourth, or fifth grade could reduce the dropout/push-out rate for low-income Black students.[10] Researchers also found that Black students in high school have a stronger expectation of going to college if they have a Black high school teacher. Dark children need teachers who not only look like them but who are engaged in an active, antiracist orientation. The conversation around the need for Black teachers must expand to having Black teachers—having all teachers, really—who teach from an abolitionist agenda. A teacher working from such an approach understands what Bernice Johnson Reagon calls "the sweetness of the struggle."[11] An antiracist approach elicits the understanding that the work of living and learning is about the solidarity created through shared struggle. Antiracist teaching is not just about acknowledging that racism exists but about consciously committing to the struggle of fighting for racial justice, and it is fundamental to abolitionist teaching. Antiracist educators seek to understand the everyday experiences of dark people living, enduring, and resisting White supremacy and White rage.

All teachers, regardless of race or ethnicity, need to know that racism is not separate from economic class and that resistance, in its various forms, is always an option. We also need to recognize the specific nuances of different types of dark oppression, recognizing that not all injustices are the same. For example, Indigenous rights are defined more by land than race, meaning that the US consistently and violently takes Indigenous land. The plight of our Indigenous students is different from that of our Latinx students. Both groups face oppression, but not the same oppression, and they have their own distinctions. All Latinx people do not face the same type of discrimination. Afro-Latinx Americans or Black Latin Americans face colorism. Latinx who are lighter-skinned do not face the same discrimination as their darker-skinned brothers and sisters. Research shows that in Latin American countries such as Bolivia, Mexico, and Colombia lighter-skinned Latinxs achieve the highest educational outcomes.[12] Black Latinxs achieve the lowest. For me, I learned this lesson firsthand when teaching and living in Miami: one of my coworker's Cuban parents decided to throw her a birthday party, but she shamefully had to tell her darker Cuban coworkers and all other dark coworkers that they were not invited because of the color of their skin.

My Black students in Homestead faced racism and poverty, while my students from Mexico met the additional barriers of racism, language, and citizenship. My Haitian students encountered these same issues, with an additional difficulty: their nationality made them Haitian while their skin color made them Black; thus, they were forced to adapt to address bigotry in both of those worlds. It is important for educators to know how deeply unjust systems affect people and their communities in unique ways, but it is also imperative to understand the intersections of injustice. Pedagogies must call out and teach students how racism, sexism, homophobia, transphobia, Islamophobia, and inequality are structural, not people behaving poorly. They must criticize the systems that perpetuate injustice, such as the educational survival complex, while pushing for equitable communities, schools, and classrooms. Antiracist education also works to undo these systems while working to create new ones built upon the collective vision and knowledge of dark folx. For educators, this work starts in the classroom, school, and school community.

COMMUNITY

A few miles from my childhood home in Rochester, New York, which was first the land of the Iroquois Nation, is the Mount Hope Cemetery, where Frederick Douglass and Susan B. Anthony are buried. Some of the most revered and feared activists and abolitionists worked and lived in my hometown. Rochester is considered the birthplace of the women's movement that is famously associated with Seneca Falls. Rochester was one of the final stops on the Underground Railroad before enslaved Black folx crossed the Niagara River into Canada for freedom. There were numerous Underground Railroad stops and stations in western New York. Harriet Tubman lived and died just sixty miles from Rochester in Auburn, New York. Frederick Douglass's *North Star* newspaper office was located at 25 East Main Street from 1847 to 1863; it was also a stop on the Underground Railroad, meaning Sojourner Truth and Harriet Tubman walked the streets of Rochester. Less than a mile from the home I grew up in stands the George Harvey Humphrey house, which is said to have tunnels and secret hiding spaces throughout it. I used to daydream as a teenager that Harriet Tubman walked down the very neighborhood streets that I called home, the Nineteenth Ward. Rochester has a rich history of activism and community building. In the 1960s, Black folx in the city had street dance parties on the weekend. During the summer months, different festivals that represented the African diaspora filled the air with good food, music, and communal love for one another's cultures. However, racial tensions in the city were high in the 1960s due to the severe housing shortage and high unemployment rate for dark people. Although at the time Rochester was known for having a robust industrial market, dark folx, when employed, were at the bottom of the pay scale, while their White coworkers got the high-paying jobs. This reality, coupled with police brutality, sparked the riot of 1962 after police beat a well-known Black store owner, Rufus Fairwell. After the riot, many groups got together to organize around the disenfranchisement that many dark folx lived prior to the uproar. Black politicians, church leaders, organizations such as FIGHT (Freedom, Independence, God, Honor, and Today), and political organizer Saul Alinsky, who wrote the book *Rules for Radicals*, came to Rochester to help efforts on the ground.[13] The work of these individuals and groups, which focused on grassroots organizing, direct-action tactics, and cooperative economic strategies, laid the foundation for the community I grew up in, which is called the Nineteenth Ward. The Nineteenth Ward knew me. Meaning, my community knew me. I was Pat and Honey Love's youngest daughter (yes, my dad's nickname was Honey). I was Gene and Johnette's baby sister (my brother is fourteen years older than me and my sister is ten years my senior). Everyone in the community knew each other and each other's business; sometimes others knew your family's business before you did. We were a close-knit community where news traveled fast and gossip even faster.

My parents were popular because they loved to throw parties. Honey was a good cook who kept cold beers in the fridge. Patty was the entertainer; she always had a joke or a story—clean or dirty—to tell. In the eyes of music enthusiasts, my parents had more than a respectable music collection; our downstairs front room was filled with records and 8-tracks. Although I went to a Catholic school, my family did not go to church. On Sunday mornings, my mother cleaned the house from top to bottom to the soundtrack of Bobby "Blue" Bland, Minnie Riperton, The Whispers, The Temptations, Gladys Knight and the Pips, Frankie Beverly & Maze, Curtis Mayfield, Patti La-Belle, James Brown, Aretha Franklin, Sam Cooke, Stevie Wonder, and Marvin Gaye. Blasting that music was my mother's way of saying, "Good morning, now clean your room." Once you heard James Brown shouting, it was time to get up. Sundays were my family's day to prepare for the week. We washed and folded clothes, cooked, and cleaned. During the week I was a latch-key kid, so I got to show off my independence before and after school. Even though I had to check in with our neighbors, the Nineteenth Ward was mine to explore. Before I could tell time I knew to leave for school after *G.I. Joe.* TV served as my entertainment and alarm clock.

In my neighborhood there were city recreation centers everywhere. Near my house alone there was a Boys & Girls Club and the Flint Street City Rec Center about five football fields away from each other. Just yards from the rec center was the Southwest Area Neighborhood Association. SWAN also had a summer camp filled with field trips, ran after-school programs, and provided family emergency services such as food, bus passes, and rental/mortgage and utility bill assistance. SWAN is the Nineteenth Ward's rock and has served the area since 1976. I would frequent SWAN, the Flint Street Rec Center, and the Boys & Girls Club throughout the week depending on what field trips or programs were being offered. As kids living in the Nineteenth Ward, we had several options and could explore our interests as we pleased.

There were after-school and summer arts programs, sports leagues, writing and poetry competitions, cooking classes, and community awards. My senior year of high school, I was named Youth Citizen of the Year for the city. At any moment my friends and I would hop into the community centers' white vans to go to museums, sporting events, plays, and movies—sometimes with only a few dollars in our pockets or no money at all. No permission slips were needed; all you had to do was call your parents, grandmother, older cousin, uncle, or aunt and let them know where and with whom you were going. No questions asked. If you were going to get back late at night, you did your homework before the van left and dropped you off at your doorstep. My mom and dad knew all the people who worked at the organizations, either through me or from their own childhoods. The grownups running the day-to-day operations of these organizations treated us like their little sisters and brothers or their kids. We were a family.

The centers were well-staffed and -resourced (art supplies, gym equipment, snacks). We were safe and loved and our talents were nurtured. SWAN, the Boys & Girls Club, and the Flint Street Rec Center were my second homes. They were extensions of my family. There were so many safe places for us to go after school, but more than that these organizations were critical to our sense of community and survival. The folx who ran them lived in the community, graduated from the same schools we attended as kids, knew our families, raised their kids in the centers, and loved our community and city. As children and young adults, we were responsible to them like we were responsible to our teachers, but it was more authentic because it was our choice to enter these spaces.

Many of my friends and I got summer jobs through these organizations. On my sixteenth birthday at 8 a.m. I started my first job at the Flint Street Rec Center as a youth counselor. The roles had changed; I was now supervising the same field trips I had gone on as a kid. I was one of the people little kids looked up to. My job gave me a sense of pride that reflected in my work and they decided to keep me on during the school year. I got a ride home every day after work from my boss, Karen, a little Italian lady who had the biggest heart, or my coworker Karl, a math whiz who could make anybody laugh. Miss James, Karl, Karen, Tony, Spanky, Twinkie, Ryan, Rick, Porter, Cookie, Tiff, Fat-Daddy, Antwan, Sally, Coach Nally, Mrs. Knight, and Eddie are the people who made sure I got home safe at night, taught me how to play basketball, mentored me, loved me, and required more of me sometimes than my parents did. I mattered to them, and the Nineteenth Ward raised me.

One major reason why my friends and I needed so much support outside of our homes is because our parents were at work. In the early 1980s, growing up in Rochester, someone in your household or a family member worked at Wegmans (a western New York grocery store chain,) Paychex (payroll and tax services), Xerox (copiers), Bausch and Lomb (one of the world's largest suppliers of eye health products), or Eastman Kodak (for most of the twentieth century, Kodak was number one in the photographic film industry). These companies had been founded and were headquartered in Rochester. At the time, because Rochester had so many booming industries, the airport was named Greater Rochester International Airport (Concourse A is called the Frederick Douglass Concourse and Concourse B is the Susan B. Anthony Concourse). Rochester was once known for its manufacturing jobs. In 1982, Kodak posted record profits and accounted for half of the city's economic activity. My mother worked at Kodak, and my dad worked as a skycap at the airport. Our strong community, which was mostly Black, was strengthened by decent-paying jobs. As it turns out, my childhood marked the end of an era for those companies, our community, the ways we learned to matter, and our survival.

THE LOSS OF CHILDHOOD

Thirty years ago, Kodak, Xerox, and Bausch and Lomb accounted for 60 percent of Rochester's workforce. In 2012 these companies made up just 6 percent.[14] In the 1980s Kodak employed sixty-two thousand mothers, brothers, fathers, daughters, grandfathers, sons, and aunts. Today, that number is less than seven thousand. In 2012 Kodak declared bankruptcy after failing to embrace the digital era, which resulted in their prices being undercut by Fujifilm. The economic downturn that led to an employment crisis was happening in my city at the same time America rebooted slavery through a war on drugs, which is code for a "War on Dark People," or what Michelle Alexander calls "the New Jim Crow."

Before the War on Drugs slogan took hold, President Richard Nixon declared drug abuse "public enemy number one." However, it is the administration of President Ronald Reagan that is responsible for the mass imprisonment of dark people. In 1980, there were less than half a million people in prison in the US. Twenty years later that number had reached close to 2.2 million.[15] President Reagan's policies emphasized imprisoning drug offenders while cutting funding for addiction treatment, privatizing prisons, and disenfranchising millions of dark Americans from their right to vote. The Clinton administration intensified the "War on Dark People" with the 1994 crime bill, which required federal prisoners to serve 85 percent of their sentence before they could be eligible for parole. President Bill Clinton also introduced the notorious "three strikes" rule, under which repeat offenders are given sentences of twenty-five years to life. Hillary Clinton called young Black men "superpredators" with "no conscience" and "no empathy." Her words were used to validate the harsh punishment of dark youth and emphasize why their lives did not matter.

However, before the Reagan and Clinton administrations, in 1973, New York, my home state, adopted the harshest mandatory minimum sentencing in the US: the Rockefeller Drug Laws. These laws, named for then New York governor Nelson Rockefeller, required judges to give drug offenders mandatory minimum sentences and were intended to prosecute drug "kingpins." Instead, for decades, they locked up tens of thousands of dark men and women for possessing drugs for their own use or for being low-level sellers or couriers. This "War on Dark People" is a reboot of slavery in the same way that, after the Civil War, slavery persisted through a system of convict leasing. The Thirteenth Amendment to the US Constitution prohibited slavery and involuntary servitude, but those convicted of a "crime" could be subject to penal labor, another form of slavery. Convict leasing allowed private companies to lease the labor of inmates. Black people were locked up and put back into slavery for loitering, not carrying proof of employment, breaking curfew, and vagrancy.

Southern states also passed laws that limited the liberties of newly freed Black people in order to maintain a labor force and an economy built on unpaid labor. For example, the Black Code laws were passed to ensure Black folx remained poor and indebted to Whites. Black Codes required Black people to obtain a license from a White person before opening a business, and Black women could not testify in court against a White man with whom she had a child (which often occurred through rape). The Black Codes also required Blacks to sign yearly labor contracts; if they refused, they could be arrested or fined. No matter what, Black folx were going to work for White folx for pennies or nothing at all. Thus, while this colored system of punishment for profit is not new, in the twentieth century, the fall of manufacturing giants, an increase in language that justifies a carceral state, and the sociopolitical power structure that keeps Whites at the top, left dark people in my hometown without a survival kit or a way to matter.

The racial disparities of the incarceration rate demonstrate another example of the human hierarchy that was codified by slavery, denies dark Americans citizenship, fails to make good on America's promises of democracy, and continually reinscribes itself as legitimate, natural, and even moral. For example, in 2016, Blacks and Hispanics made up 71 percent of the US prison population, even though these groups made up just one-quarter of the population.[16] More than 1.5 million children have a parent in prison, and more than 8.3 million have a parent under correctional supervision.[17] I would be remiss if I did not point out that 37 percent of female and 28 percent of male prisoners have monthly incomes of less than $600 before their arrest. A quarter of women in state prison have a history of mental illness, while 80 percent of all women in jails are mothers.[18] In New York, 18.2 percent of women inmates are HIV-positive. And, all too often, incarcerated women are survivors of physical abuse (47 percent) or sexual abuse (39 percent), with many surviving both. Upward of 90 percent of women in prison for killing a man were abused by the man they killed.[19] To add insult to injury, dark women also face extreme amounts of violence in prisons.

Our juvenile justice system is no better. According to a 2016 report by the Sentencing Project, youth incarceration had declined over the previous decade; however, racial disparities had increased. Dark youth are still more likely than White youth to be committed to a juvenile facility. Hispanic youth are 61 percent more likely than White youth to be committed, Black youth are four times more likely, and Native Americans are three times more likely. The vulnerability of being young and dark alongside the multiple intersections of being human intensifies the unjust nature of the justice system. For example, transgender and gender-nonconforming youth are more likely to be deported. Undocumented youth experience high levels of criminalization, poverty, and profiling by law enforcement at schools. The educational survival complex adopts the school-to-prison pipeline because we all live in a carceral state, increasing deportation for queer undocumented youth. In general, gay, transgender, and gender-nonconforming dark youth are overrepresented in the juvenile justice system. Our most vulnerable youth are walking targets for White rage inside and outside the walls of schools.

One of the most cruel and inhumane examples of our violent and racially discriminatory justice system is the case of Kalief Browder, who committed suicide at his parents' home after spending three years in custody in one of the most notorious jail complexes in the US— New York's Rikers Island—for allegedly stealing a backpack. Arrested at age sixteen, he spent two of those three years in solitary confinement, twenty-three hours a day, locked in a cell, alone. Because Kalief could not afford an attorney, and his parents could not post the $3,000 bail, his spirit was murdered in the solitude of his innocence. Kalief refused all plea deals, even one that would have secured his immediate release, because he knew he was innocent. His court-appointed public defender, Brendan O'Meara, felt the case was "relatively straightforward," but the Bronx District Attorney's office was extremely backlogged.[20] Kalief was beaten by officers and attacked by inmates in jail; he tried to commit suicide several times.

After three years of abuse and being treated like a caged wild animal, Kalief was released when prosecutors dropped the charges, citing a lack of evidence. Once released, Kalief tried to put the past behind him, but the trauma of being in jail followed him around even in his home. His family members describe him as living in fear of being attacked like he was in jail, and checking all the windows in the house to make sure they were locked before going to sleep. He was even hospitalized in a psychiatric ward at Harlem Hospital Center. Then, at the age of twenty-two, Kalief hanged himself at his parents' home in the Bronx.

What happened to Kalief Browder is beyond tragic, even more so because it is common. It helps us sleep at night to think that Kalief's story is an anomaly, and that his death was caused by multiple unfortunate events. But the reality is that dark innocent bodies are held in prison for no other reason than being dark and poor, and therefore disposable. Between 2014 and 2015, six counties in the state of California spent $37.5 million to jail people whose cases were dismissed or never filed.[21] Poor Black folx ages eighteen to twenty-nine typically receive higher bail amounts than any other group. Unable to afford bail, many people plead guilty. Only 4 percent of convictions result from trials. Civil and human rights groups around the country are organizing to reform and abolish the prison-industrial complex and the bail system that pushes families and communities apart. Through their work, perhaps those like Kalief—dark bodies who can never return whole with their souls intact—can have the opportunity to feel like home is where they matter.

HOME

When I was young, the most important measure of success was leaving Rochester. Our parents, grandparents, teachers, and community role models all said the same thing: "You have to leave this place." This was because Rochester's "homeplace" had collapsed. Described by bell hooks, "homeplace" is a space where Blacks folx truly matter to each other, where souls are nurtured, comforted, and fed. Homeplace is a community, typically led by women, where White power and the damages done by it are healed by loving Blackness and restoring dignity. She argues that "homeplace" is a site of resistance. Understanding the gutting of dark communities' homeplaces is critical to a teacher's analysis of the community in which he or she teaches.

For example, in 1985, there were twenty-six murders in the city of Rochester and 1,072 robberies. By 1990, there were forty murders in the city and 1,254 robberies. In 1995, fifty-three murders and 1,576 robberies took place. In 2002, the *New York Times* ran a story with the headline "Mean Streets of New York? Increasingly, They're Found in Rochester." The article stated that 93 percent of school-age children lived in poverty, and only a quarter of high school freshmen lasted the four years to graduation. In 2013, Rochester had the lowest graduation rate in the state at 50 percent, with pockets of concentrated poverty throughout the city. Currently, Rochester is one of the poorest cities in America, with more people living at or below the federal poverty level than any other city with similar demographics.[22] The typical family of four in Rochester lives off $11,925 or less a year, which is classified as extreme poverty. And according to a 2017 study by researchers at Stanford University, the Rochester City School District had the lowest academic growth among the eleven thousand school districts.[23]

Rochester is not an anomaly; many US cities mirror these statistics. And just as Rochester did not become riddled by crime, high unemployment, drugs, and low-performing schools overnight, neither did Detroit, Chicago, Cincinnati, St. Louis, or Atlanta. White rage methodically destroyed these cities for their dark residents in the form of Jim Crow, school desegregation, urban development or gentrification (which is code for removing and displacing dark bodies), the War on Drugs, mass incarceration, police brutality, school rezoning and closings, redlining (from 1934 to 1968 the Federal Housing Administration denied dark people home loans), globalization of the US manufacturing industry, vanishing public sector jobs, and the educational survival complex. What is truly amazing is that dark folx have always found ways to survive it all. Despite the fact that almost all the sites of resistance created by early abolitionists, teachers, community organizers, civil rights leaders, and, ultimately, dark women, have been gradually and methodically destroyed by White rage. This is why homeplace is needed, because it is a place that honors the emotional, physical, spiritual, and financial struggle of living under what hooks calls "the brutal reality of racial apartheid" in the US and finding one's humanity within the struggle against it.[24] FIST was my homeplace. Mrs. Johnson's and Mr. Clayton's classrooms were my homeplace. The community centers were my homeplace. And my home, with a mother who did everything in her power to protect me from the realities of racism and armed me with the tools to survive in hopes that I would one day thrive, was my homeplace.

THRIVE

For dark folx, thriving cannot happen without a community that is deeply invested in racial uplift, human and workers' rights, affordable housing, food and environmental justice, land rights, free or affordable healthcare, healing, joy, cooperative economic strategies, and high political participation that is free of heteropatriarchy, homophobia, Islamophobia, transphobia, sexism, ageism, and the politics of respectability. These structural ideologies police who is worthy of dignity within our communities. One of the most prolific, courageous, intellectual thinkers and acute political organizers for social change of all time is Ella Baker, though her work is rarely discussed. She worked from the premise that "strong people don't need strong leaders." She devoted her life to grassroots organizing and critiqued not only racism but also sexism and classism. Baker's strategic mind was fundamental in establishing and guiding organizations such as In Friendship, the National Association for the Advancement of Colored People, the Southern Christian Leadership Conference, the Student Nonviolent Coordinating Committee, Crusade for Citizenship, and the Southern Conference Education Fund. She organized for the Mississippi Freedom Democratic Party, and later in her life she supported the Free Angela Davis campaign, the Puerto Rican Independence Movement, and ending apartheid in South Africa.

Baker was critical of charismatic male leaders, or the singular charismatic leader who did not empower people with the tools to transform their lived conditions. She believed in the power of oppressed people and communities to create pathways to leadership that were decentralized and not hierarchical. She wanted people to understand just how strong and brilliant they were both individually and collectively. Baker was driven by the idea of a radical democratic practice in which the oppressed, excluded, and powerless became active in positions of power with decision-making opportunities.[25] This idea is why FIST made such an impact on me; it was a site of resistance where I had power and made decisions that affected my friends and my community.

In a 1970 interview, Baker said, "In my organizational work, I have never thought in terms of my 'making a contribution.' I just thought of myself as functioning where there was a need."[26] In the book *Ella Baker and the Black Freedom Movement: A Radical Democratic Vision*, author Barbara Ransby documents how Baker, as a member of the Harlem Adult Education Experiment during the 1930s, was the main facilitator for bringing together different sectors of the Black community, collapsing generational barriers, and creating spaces for people to exchange their goods and services. Baker invited the most prominent speakers of her time to encourage youth to be active participants in their world. She aimed to instill a sense of power in young people by teaching them to critically analyze their world and to articulate their own beliefs about injustice. According to Ransby, Baker believed "that education and the exchange and dissemination of ideas could make a difference in people's lives."[27] Baker knew that her work as an educator was also tied with the fight for economic justice: "People cannot be free until there is enough work in this land to give everyone a job."[28] She worked toward organizing Black economic power and ran voter registration drives. But what made Baker such a powerhouse was her relentless development of new and young activists. She wanted to harness the ambition, passion, creativity, rebelliousness, courage, and openness of youth to confront injustice. Baker helped organize one of the most important organizations of the civil rights movement: the Student Nonviolent Coordinating Committee.

SNCC's conception is a testament to Baker's leadership style. More than three hundred students, inspired by the civil rights movement, were invited to a planning meeting at Shaw University in Raleigh, North Carolina, where Baker had graduated as valedictorian. Baker planned the meeting with deliberation and precision. For example, she made sure that those who were politically engaged were at the center of deliberations, not the so-called experts. She urged everyone in attendance to meet with Southern students who were Black and less politically experienced to make sure they learned the fundamental skills needed to organize. She made sure that those in attendance knew that "the leadership for the South had to be a southern leadership."[29] At the meeting, she also encouraged closed-door strategy sessions where young people could express themselves and discuss policy without reporters watching. Her second reason for the closed-door sessions was to prevent any one student from stealing the spotlight for the work of the conference. Baker did not like grandstanding. She wanted the students to get organized, and she wanted adults and young people to work together from a vision for participatory democracy. From this meeting, without Baker making any unilateral decisions, SNCC was created. SNCC members would go on to lead the Freedom Riders, organize voter registration drives, and shape the March on Washington for Jobs and Freedom. A true measure of SNCC's participatory democracy is how many Black women held prominent positions in the civil rights movement and government because of their training and participation in SNCC, including Bernice Reagon, Diane Nash, Fannie Lou Hamer, Unita Blackwell, and Eleanor Holmes Norton.

Baker approached all her work through participatory democracy, which rejected top-down, hierarchal, male-centered leadership. Participatory democracy uplifts voices that have been deliberately placed in the margins and seeks to organize, strategize, and mobilize through consensus building. Baker wanted everyday people to resist oppression through their collective power, which, she argued, was a more sustainable and transformative method to attain freedom. Through meetings, reading groups, debates, and strategy sessions, everyday people were centered in their communities for the fight for justice.

Baker never wrote an organizing manual; she led by her actions. Her power was subtle yet deliberate. She stressed grassroots organizing and mass mobilization. Participatory democracy's egalitarian structure allowed for women to move from second-class status to leaders within the civil rights movement. White women who were members of SNCC learned the practices of participatory democracy from Baker and other organizers. Many organizations of the women's movement, which was founded on the heels of the civil rights movement, centered participatory democracy as the leadership model. Baker's participatory democracy, dependent on individual citizens learning and growing together, focused on a layered agenda for justice that utilized everyone's skill sets to emphasize self-worth and collective liberation. In sum, Baker's philosophy of community is how dark folx move from surviving to thriving, so that we matter to one another and the world. We cannot pursue educational freedom or any type of justice without a model of democracy that empowers all. We all thrive when everyday people resist, when everyday people find their voice, when everyday people demand schools that are students' homeplaces, and when everyday people understand that loving darkness is our path to humanity.

Taking the lead from Baker, abolitionist teaching is built on the cultural wealth of students' communities and creating classrooms in parallel with those communities aimed at facilitating interactions where people matter to each other, fight together in the pursuit of creating a homeplace that represents their hopes and dreams, and resist oppression all while building a new future. Growing up, I had multiple homeplaces that valued me, all of me, all the time. Looking back, I see that these spaces were abolitionist spaces in that they protected my humanity, my dignity, and not only told me I was powerful but taught me how to be powerful. These abolitionist spaces loved Blackness and understood that, to be dark, you must give this world hell to survive.

CHAPTER 4

GRIT, ZEST, AND RACISM (THE HUNGER GAMES)

They aren't "bad kids." They're just trying to survive bad circumstances.

—MICHELLE OBAMA, *Becoming*

BAIT AND SWITCH: CIVICS EDUCATION TO CHARACTER EDUCATION

Critical thinking, problem solving, social and emotional intelligence, zest, self-advocacy, grit, optimism, self-control, curiosity, and gratitude are the characteristics school officials, politicians, policymakers, educational consulting firms, curriculum writers, education researchers, and corporate school reformers prepackage and sell to educators and parents of dark children. For most schools in the US, especially schools with a large majority of low-income and dark students, their mission statements, weekly blogs, and fundraising materials are plastered with these racially coded feel-good, work-hard, and take-responsibility-for-my-actions buzzwords that make up character education. Character education has been around since the development of education in America; the founding fathers of public education (Horace Mann, William McGuffey, and Benjamin Franklin) wanted to teach morality in schools.[1] However, the explosion of character education arose during the 1980s and 1990s when private, large-scale programs such as the Heartwood Program and Character Counts! infiltrated public education. These programs, with no formal evaluation of their success rates, were bought by public schools everywhere on the belief that their growing student bodies of dark and poor students lacked good character. Presidents Bill Clinton and George W. Bush each tripled funding for character education during their administrations.[2] At face value, character education seems harmless, and I am sure we can all agree that children need good qualities to be successful in life, regardless of how you define success, but character education is anti-Black and it has replaced civics education in our schools. Students no longer learn how to be informed and active citizens, which is key to democracy; instead, they learn now how to comply and recite affirmations about their grit.

A robust civics education should include discussions focused on current events, opportunities for students to participate in school governance, media literacy, and classroom instruction on government, history, law, economics, and geography.[3] However, the 2010 National Assessment of Education Progress surveyed twelfth graders from around the US and found that 70 percent of students self-reported having never once written a letter to give an opinion or help solve a problem. In the same study, 56 percent reported never having gone on a field trip or having had an outside speaker come to their class.[4] In 2011, fewer than half of all the eighth graders in the US knew the purpose of the Bill of Rights.[5] We are now living with the repercussions of our citizens having low media literacy (everything is "fake news") and not being able to solve problems that impact us all collectively (e.g., climate change, living wages, and food scarcity).

Civics education scholar Meira Levinson calls our current and intentional lack of educating our youth with the skills and the knowledge to be a part of democracy, the "civic empowerment gap."[6] There is a civic empowerment gap because the rich have all the political influence and civics education is no longer a space that teaches youth how to petition, protest, speak in public, solve social issues with groups of people from diverse backgrounds, and commit to acts of civil disobedience.[7] Our students are now taught with the world crumbling around them to pay their taxes, vote, volunteer, and have good character, which is code for comply, comply, comply. Dark children are told that their good character is dependent on how much they obey. However, history tells us that dark folx' humanity is dependent on how much they disobey and fight for justice, which can sometimes be a losing battle. So, civics for dark folx is our life. Yes, I agree with Levinson's concept of the "civic empowerment gap," but nothing can ever measure how dark people fight injustice, find ways to love, and build community, which makes simply being a dark person a civics project.

TRAYVON MARTIN

On February 26, 2012, seventeen-year-old Trayvon Martin displayed all these characteristics by which school officials claim to measure, rate, and rank dark children, but it could not save his life. Trayvon was on the phone with Rachel Jeantel, his close friend, when he noticed George Zimmerman, a self-appointed neighborhood watch captain, and told her that a "creepy White cracker" was following him. From Rachel's testimony, one can glean that Trayvon was keenly aware of his surroundings, and that Zimmerman made him very uncomfortable. On the night of his death, Trayvon's grit was tested and measured, not in a lab but by White rage—and not many pass this test. The character education he received by virtue of being a Black boy in America informed him that he would need to fight to stay alive. This is the character education and grit that researchers cannot measure in a lab and do not understand.

The Character Lab, a nonprofit organization cofounded in 2016 by psychologist Angela Duckworth, who popularized the term "grit"; Dave Levin, the cofounder of KIPP public charter schools; and Dominic Randolph, head of Riverdale Country School in the Bronx, define social and emotional intelligence as the ability "to understand your own and others' feelings and emotions and then to use this understanding to inform your decisions and actions."[8] They go on to add that people with high social and emotional intelligence find solutions when they are in conflict with someone, can quickly adapt to social situations, can show respect for others' feelings, and are less likely to engage in violence. Trayvon Martin quickly adapted to his environment by determining that Zimmerman was a threat—a superpredator—and by recalling the fear that dark people know all too well based on centuries of White rage. Trayvon did not just say that a man was following him or a White man was following him: he called Zimmerman a "creepy White cracker." Trayvon was conscious and alert that this situation was about race, and the history of creepy White men following dark people. He was being racially profiled, and he knew it.

Trayvon was not the only one on the phone that night. Zimmerman called 911 and told the dispatcher that Trayvon looked "suspicious": "This guy looks like he is up to no good or he is on drugs or something." He later told the dispatcher on the same call, "He's got his hand in his waistband. And he's a Black man." Trayvon could not hear Zimmerman, but he knew his life was in danger. He started to run. "Shit, he's running," Zimmerman told the dispatcher. The dispatcher then asked Zimmerman if he was following the young Black man. He replied, "Yeah." The dispatcher told him, "Okay, we don't need you to do that." Zimmerman said, "Okay." The dispatcher reassured Zimmerman that the police were on their way.[9]

That night, Trayvon was walking home from the neighborhood convenience store carrying a bag of Skittles, a cell phone, and an iced tea and wearing a hoodie. By the time the police arrived, Trayvon was dead. But Trayvon fought for his life; all the grit, self-control, critical thinking, problem solving, and self-advocacy were not enough. He problem-solved that his best option was to run, drawing on a history of White violence toward dark bodies. When attacked by Zimmerman, he advocated for his life. The night of the murder, Zimmerman was treated for a fractured nose and cuts to the back of his head. By fighting for his life, Trayvon showed his grit and tried his best to stay alive. He stood his ground.

HUNGER GAMES

The Character Lab defines grit as "perseverance and passion for long-term goals."[10] Revising an essay repeatedly or not quitting a sport in the middle of the season are examples of gritty behavior, according to the Character Lab. But what if your long-term goal is fighting racism? Is four hundred years long enough? We have rebelled, fought, conformed, pleaded with the courts, marched, protested, boycotted, created timeless art that reflects our lives, and become president of the country that disposes of us with little to no relief of our oppression. *Is this not grit?* I take issue with this line of research focused on dark children's behavior by way of examining their character "strengths" and "weaknesses" because we live in a racist, sexist, Islamophobic, patriarchal, homophobic, transphobic, and xenophobic world where grit is not enough to fight these systems. Yes, it is needed, but to insist that dark children need, do not have, and can function on those characteristics alone is misleading, naïve, and dangerous.

Measuring dark students' grit while removing no institutional barriers is education's version of *The Hunger Games*. It is adults overseeing which dark children can beat the odds, odds put in place and maintained by an oppressive system. In the state of Georgia, the Governor's Office of Student Achievement gives out an actual award to schools called "Beating the Odds." The award is calculated by "compar[ing] schools' ability to teach based on student characteristics that are 'outside the school's control.' Race, ethnicity, disabilities, English fluency, economic 'disadvantage' and transience" are all considered.[11] In Georgia, only 40 percent of schools beat the odds.[12] So, the state acknowledges that there are barriers that hinder students' educational growth, but instead of eliminating English-only testing or funding education fully, it tests dark children specifically against odds they and their families did not create, knowing they cannot win.

This type of educational *Hunger Games* propaganda leads educators to believe that the key to "success" for dark children lies in improving their grit and zest "levels." The Character Lab defines zest as "an approach to life that is filled with excitement and energy." How do you measure zest when forces you cannot stop with a pep talk and a colorful graph systemically suck the life out of you? Dark students being gritty, full of excitement and energy, reciting self-improvement statements, and displaying social and emotional intelligence does not stop them from being killed in the streets or spirit-murdered in the classroom; these are their odds. It does nothing for kids growing up poor, who experience the stresses and traumas of poverty. Research has shown that the stress of poverty and adversity alters brain functions. It is called "toxic stress." Children who experience prolonged adversities—poverty, chronic neglect, the US government separating children from their parents, violence, physical or emotional abuse—suffer great impact on their ability to learn. Specifically, according to the Centers for Disease Control and Prevention, research has shown that children who experience high levels of toxic stress display impaired social and emotional understanding, along with learning disabilities and potential early death.[13] Researchers believe that, because toxic stress creates neurobiological transformation in children, it should be seen and treated as a national health crisis.

Dark children, especially those who are experiencing or have experienced toxic stress, do not need their grit measured or their character examined by researchers or school officials. They need culturally relevant therapy that teaches age-appropriate stress-reduction practices and they need mentors who understand what being a critical mentor means (see the work of Torie Weiston-Serdan). Students need youth-centered programs like FIST; Young, Gifted, and Black (Oakland, California); and Kuumba Lynx (Chicago). They need health services in the schools that service their community. Students need paid internships and career planning courses. Schools need healthy foods programs and urban gardens. Every community needs a Children's Defense Fund Freedom School. These schools have been models for teaching social change for more than fifty years, built in response to the educational survival complex after Black schools closed around the country in reaction to *Brown v. Board of Education*. Dark children need an end to the school-to-prison pipeline through the decriminalization of schools by removing security guards, metal detectors, and police and with deliberate speed, inserting restorative justice and mindful practices in schools and communities alike. Every child needs a counselor or therapist. In order to make mental health as important as education, the two must and should work in tandem. However, we have to address that school counselor shortage. The American School Counselor Association suggests a ratio of

250 students to each counselor. In the 2014–2015 school year, only Vermont, Wyoming, and New Hampshire met that ratio.[14] The rest of the forty-seven states did not even come close to that number: for example, Arizona 924:1, California 760:1, Michigan 727:1, Florida 485:1, and Georgia 484:1.[15]

If education is going to deal with trauma, we must recognize the trauma of our teachers. Educators need trauma sensitive training and free or affordable therapy for themselves. Schools of educational psychology should create degrees that help school counselors understand the human development needed to be a teacher. Teachers need to be taught how to question Whiteness and White supremacy, how to check and deal with their White emotions of guilt and anger, and how these all impact their classrooms. Only after unpacking and interrogating Whiteness, White teachers—and, really, all teachers—must unpack how Whiteness functions in their lives; then they can stand in solidarity with their students' communities for social change. Teachers must demand the end of high-stakes testing and the yelling of slogans at dark children, such as "knowledge is power," "work hard," "be nice," and "no excuses" because all you need is grit. And, lastly, teachers need to mobilize to fight systemic inequities and the educational survival complex.

HISTORY, TRAUMA, AND GRIT

According to reports, approximately 62 percent of all children come to school every day experiencing some type of trauma.[16] As upsetting as this sounds, and is, scientists now know that trauma is passed down. For some of us, trauma is in our DNA. The scientific phenomenon is known as "epigenetic inheritance." A recent study of Holocaust survivors found that their children had an increased likelihood of stress disorders. Our genes constantly adapt to their environment through chemical tags, which switch genes off and on. Scientists found that Dutch women who were pregnant during a severe famine at the end of the Second World War birthed girls at above-average risk of developing schizophrenia. Thus, research shows that people who live through high levels of toxic stress alter the genes of their children and, therefore, the lives they will lead.

Measuring students' grit and zest, and reminding them that there are "no excuses," sounds like an easy fix for oppression, but telling dark children that they need to pull themselves up by their bootstraps and achieve on their own merit is not a new approach; it is short-sighted and, in actuality, racist thinking.

It should come as no surprise that the KIPP charter school network and the inventor of the character growth card—all aspects of the educational survival complex—allowed Duckworth to test her grit theory on children. Dave Levin, the cofounder of KIPP, clings to the field of positive psychology, which declares that success in college and life can be predicted by testing for positive character strengths such as grit, zest, gratitude, and social intelligence. He introduced the field of education to the character growth card and character performance assessments (CPAs). According to a 2014 article by Jeffrey Aaron Snyder in the *New Republic*:

> When Levin first hit on the idea of a character report card in 2007, he envisioned that students would eventually graduate with both a GPA and a CPA, or character point average. In Levin's conception, the CPA would be a valuable tool for admissions officers and corporate human resources managers who would be delighted to know which applicants had scored highest on items such as grit, optimism, and zest.[17]

What Levin makes clear in his obsession with positive psychology and measuring the character of dark and poor children—KIPP's primary student population—is his belief that dark children can be better controlled and better workers if their character is tracked throughout their lives. Levin's thinking can be traced back hundreds of years to "good" White folx who thought that, given the "proper" education and learning environment, dark children (Native Americans, African Americans, Chinese Americans, Japanese Americans, and Mexican Americans) could be taught how to be less barbaric and more White. Never fully White, of course, but White enough to be less threatening, less outspoken, and more task-driven (gritty), so that nothing could supersede White economic demands for labor.

According to historian Robert G. Lee, Asian Americans were stereotyped into different categories by the level of threat to the "American national family" during the 1960s and 1970s.[18] These labels included "coolie," a servile Asian worker willing to work countless hours for low wages; "deviant," someone with sexual freedom that threatened the morality of White families; "yellow peril," or the idea that Asian immigrants would invade the US; and "model minority," pristine Asian immigrants and Asian Americans who, as gifted students, business owners, engineers, and apolitical married men and women, were grateful to be in America and did not want to discuss or challenge the brutal mistreatment of Asian immigrants in the past, such as the Los Angeles mob lynching in 1871 of twenty-two Chinese men. Journalist Jeff Guo argues that the success of Asian Americans is not solely due to educational achievements but also to the fact that White Americans stopped being so explicitly racist toward them because they believed the model-minority trope.[19] America bought into the character scorecard of Asian Americans years ago. In 1974, writer Frank Chin said, regarding the model-minority image, "Whites love us because we're not Black."[20] It is important to note that Asian Americans who do not fit within the model-minority stereotype are discriminated against and face racism daily. The character scoring never stops, and it is also an element of anti-Blackness.

According to Snyder, using the KIPP growth scorecard protocol, Bernie Madoff (the con man who ran the largest Ponzi scheme in US history at $64.8 billion) would have been an exceptional student, displaying hard work, charm, and zest for life. Donald Trump unsuccessfully ran for president for over fifteen years before taking office in 2017. By definition, Donald Trump is gritty, hard-working, and demonstrates perseverance. His tenacity in his quest to become

president should be celebrated by grit enthusiasts. How Trump became president—through ruthless power, White privilege, Russian
interference, misogyny, and racism—does not matter to such believ-
ers because he has "perseverance and passion for long-term goals."[21]

In the world of grit, the ideas of love, kindness, thoughtfulness,
courage, honesty, integrity, and justice are rarely discussed, nor is the
idea of epigenetic inheritance. In her book *Grit*, Angela Duckworth
reconciles the points that someone can be a "gritty villain" and that
"altruistic purpose is not an absolute requirement of grit."[22] Therefore,
she concludes that interest, purpose, and hope are needed for gritty
people to do good in the world. She argues that grit depends largely
on hope:

> Grit depends on a different kind of hope. It rests on the expecta-
> tion that our own efforts can improve our future. *I have a feeling
> tomorrow will be better* is different from *I resolve to make tomorrow
> better*. The hope that gritty people have has nothing to do with
> luck and everything to do with getting up again.[23]

This statement does not reflect and is out of touch with the real
world and what it means to be dark, poor, and surviving. There are
millions of people who work fifty to seventy hours a week, some at
two or three jobs, but they cannot afford to pay their bills because
the minimum wage does not cover the rising cost of living in the US.
They keep getting up again and again, working, but they remain in
poverty. This ceaseless cycle is no fault of theirs; the working poor
are among the grittiest. They persevere for the long-term goal of
their children's education. They hope that life can and will be better
for the next generation. That is the grit of dark people. They work
endlessly for the next generation and the next day with resolve, purpose, hope, faith, and a desire for their children to thrive one day
off the labor of their grit. For dark people, being gritty means being solution-oriented, it means finding a way out of no way because
you understand what is needed to solve the issues you are facing but
lack the power and resources. Redirecting power and resources is a

primary focus of abolitionist teaching and the goal of educators and individuals concerned about educational justice, rather than measuring grit or appraising dark children's characters in toxic environments or while they're living with the stress of being young and dark. Our focus must shift instead to protecting our students' potential.

PROTECTING POTENTIAL

Just as I placed my fingers on the computer keys to write this section, I received a text message from a former student, Mark. Now a tenth grader, Mark was in my middle school Hip-Hop for Social Justice course. Mark had called me a few weeks earlier to tell me his mother had passed away. Though she had been incarcerated for most of his life, Mark loved his mom and wanted her to get the help she needed to beat her drug addiction. Mark lives with his grandmother and grandfather; his grandfather is frequently in and out of the hospital. In replying to my text from a few days before when I was just checking in, he wrote back: "I haven't really been feeling it. But I gotta keep pushin." I asked Mark if he had some time to get together for lunch so we could talk, and I would not take no for an answer. He finally gave in, but he wanted me to know that "also, Im just really busy rn [right now] with home and a lot of things. Including just mentally tired." I would say it is ironic, reading his words while critiquing the concept of grit. Most teachers have taught a student like Mark—some have taught dozens of Marks—students enduring extreme physical, emotional, and mental fatigue and tackling roadblocks that a child cannot move alone.

To be honest, in some ways my childhood mirrored Mark's. And, yes, I am gritty for overcoming obstacles. I made a success of myself despite a stressful home life, but that is because of my teachers, my brother, my sister, my basketball coaches, my athletic director, my mentors, FIST, my first boss and my coworkers at the Rec Center in Rochester, the staff at the Boys & Girls Club, my high school friends, and everyday people in my neighborhood who protected me, protected my grit, protected my zest, and protected my potential. They were my village.

I checked in with my high school basketball coach, Mike Nally, every morning before school started. I knew his family and that he wanted for me what he wanted for his own kids. However, he understood that my circumstances were different, so we discussed race and racism and talked almost daily about what he called "my ticket out" of Rochester. My high school athletic director, Judi Knight, became my second mom when my own mother left to get the help she needed. She also became my advocate. My high school math teacher, Miss Val, gave me extra-credit work to improve my grades, tutored me after school, came to my games, and drove me home. Those rides home were filled with conversations about college, the pressures of high school, and how good a student I was becoming (and I needed to hear that).

My coworkers Karl and Karen gave me rides home every night after work. Karen, my first boss, who hired me on my sixteenth birthday to start work at 8 a.m., did my taxes and taught me how to budget my money. Mrs. James at the Boys & Girls Club was one of my very first Black woman role models besides Mrs. Johnson. The passion Mrs. James had for every kid who walked through her door was infectious because it was so sincere. My twenty-six-year-old sister stepped in as my guardian to advocate on my behalf and demanded that my high school track my progress with biweekly report cards to ensure I was on track for graduation and college. My brother, who worked at McDonald's, would bring food to the basketball court around 1 a.m. on the weekends to make sure I was fed and safe. My older best friends asked their parents if I could stay at their houses, sometimes for days, told me to do my homework, and made sure I did not repeat their mistakes. And so many others: All the guys on the corners—yes, some were drug dealers—who made sure I got home safely at night from the courts. The local corner store cashiers who let me go when I was short a few cents. My mother and father who taught me early on in life, so that when they were not there, I was still giving this world hell. All the free summer programs that took my friends and me around New York State, exposing us to a life beyond our neighborhood. And all the countless folx in my zip code (14611) who believed in me and my dreams and poured their own dreams into mine because theirs had been deferred.

I am beyond grateful for all the people who protected me because of my gift: basketball. I would not have crossed paths with these amazing individuals if I could not put a ball through a hoop. My senior year of high school I was six-foot-one and averaged more than thirty points a game. I had a talent that was valued by society, and women's basketball was presented to me as my only option for successes (though still not as valued as men's basketball). But looking back, I wonder about the multitudes of kids in my neighborhood who could not put a ball through a hoop. My freshman year, more than five hundred ninth graders entered the doors of my high school with me; fewer than two hundred graduated. I graduated because I had what felt like an entire football team blocking for me. I survived; I am now thriving because my grit and zest were protected, nurtured, and cherished not only by teachers and coaches but also by my community. The grit and zest that I was born with, that my ancestors passed down to me, and that Black culture embodies were never taken away from me as a child, or depleted to a point where I did not want to fight this world any longer. I left Rochester as a seventeen-year-old Black girl with my spirit intact, which made all the difference in my life.

LEVERAGE, INTERSECTIONS, AND LIFT

Protecting children's potential is not an easy lift, and it cannot be done episodically. My protectors were not just people who volunteered once a year with children from low-income neighborhoods or donated canned goods to the local food bank for a community service project; they were committed to building a relationship with me, my family, and my community in ways that were authentic and honored my knowledge of growing up Black and a woman in America. They respected my family; they also respected my community and saw the value in both. Even though my home and community were broken, they saw me beyond my trauma. They asked about my mother and father and knew how much I needed them to do well so that I could do well. They lived in my community or understood me, so I did not have to explain my community's shortcomings as a young adult. I remember Coach Nally, who is White, explaining how he had grown up in Rochester and how the city had changed over the years and how racism impacted the city. He never ran from hard conversations about racism, and he always discussed and confronted the imbalance of power and privilege within our relationship.

Mrs. Knight, who is also White, would tell me about her difficult childhood and the struggles of her mother, but always with the understanding that while our life stories may have intersected and overlapped, that my darkness was a factor that further complicated my life, while her Whiteness eased hers. Mrs. James, the commanding director of the Boys & Girls Club and a Black woman, demanded more from me than I knew I had. I never, ever wanted to let Mrs. James down, and still, to this day, strive to make her proud. She was my mother and grandmother all in one. On hot summer days, with 150 kids running around, just the sound of her voice over the loudspeaker saying "Freeze" suddenly turned our feet to cement and taped our mouths shut. The young guys like Karl, Fat-Daddy, Tony, Spanky, Brian, and Eddie let me play in all the boys' basketball leagues and dared anyone, especially another boy, to say anything about it. They took me home, picked me up, and made sure I was safe. I never felt threatened by these men.

These individuals were not only benevolent, but they also recognized the intersections of our relationships. These men knew they had to protect me. Fat-Daddy would tell all the boys that if they messed with me or picked on me, they would have to deal with him. White folx in my life used their position, power, and privilege to negotiate space and opportunities for me. My senior year of high school, I needed to raise my GPA and retake a shop class that I had failed as a freshman. Mrs. Knight made a few calls and enrolled me in night classes and an additional English class.

I share these details of my life not to echo a cheesy movie like *The Blind Side* with a White savior, because there are no saviors. There is only a village, a community, and a goal: protecting children's potential. My homeplace. This work is hard, frustrating, and some-times seemingly depressing. One person cannot do all the heavy lifting. I needed critical mentors, math tutors, SAT tutors, coaches, bodyguards, rides home, a job, financial literacy, college prep, ther-apy, and folx to make calls, schedule meetings, run interference, and leverage their power and privilege on my behalf. These folx knew I was a good kid in a mad city. I was not just a kid who could play bas-ketball; my multiple identities made me vulnerable and I needed to be protected, mentored, and employed.

Although my beloved community was plagued with gangs, drugs, violence, and senseless killings, I felt safe walking home in the middle of the night, at school, at home, at the rec center and the Boys & Girls Club, and in late-night rides home from a game or work with a group of boys and men. My community put me on their shoulders, understood their male and White privilege, and leveraged their po-sitions and power to do the heavy lifting of getting me off to college with my spirit whole and intact.

INTERSECTIONS OF PROTECTION

As grateful as I am, it saddens me that it took so many people to get one little dark girl out of economic and racial isolation (the 'hood). My story is the kind that makes people feel good, the story people use to claim that the system works. But beyond such sadly rare so-called feel-good stories, we need to focus on the little dark girls and boys whom no one protects because they cannot put a ball through a hoop, lay someone out on the football field, or become a successful rapper or singer.

I live in Atlanta, home of Coca-Cola, Home Depot, Chick-fil-A, Delta, CNN, and Dr. Martin Luther King Jr. Atlanta is also one of the largest hubs for human trafficking. The city's wealthiest residents make twenty times more than the residents at the lowest income level, a wider gap than in any other US city in 2014, 2015, and 2017 (in 2016, Atlanta was third, behind Boston and New Orleans).[24] Ac-cording to a 2013 report, Atlanta has lower rates of mobility than any developed country.[25] Poor kids in Atlanta have a 4.5 percent chance of climbing the mobility income ladder to reach the top fifth of earners in the city.[26]

The city's public transportation is lackluster and longtime Atlanta residents are being displaced, as affordable housing is scarce. The title of a 2016 article in *Atlanta Magazine* says it all: "Has Intown Atlanta Lost Affordable Housing for Good?"[27] The huge income gap ensures that individuals and families cannot afford to live in the new luxury apartment buildings. In 2016, Atlanta was named one of America's top "murder capital" cities after having seventy-four murders in 2015. Atlanta also tops the list of US cities with the most infrastructure concerns. (You may remember a major bridge collapsing in Atlanta in the spring of 2017; thankfully no one was hurt.) Lastly, Atlanta is known to the world as an economic powerhouse. Big businesses flock to Atlanta, and the city is a driver of popular culture, especially Black popular culture, such as rap music and the TV show *Atlanta*. Atlanta is known as a "City Too Busy to Hate" and the "Black mecca." However, 80 percent of Atlanta's Black children, 43 percent of Latinx children, and 29 percent of Asian children live in communities with a high concentration of poverty.[28] The unemployment rate for Black folx in the city is 22 percent, twice the city's overall rate.

As far as education goes, according to the Governor's Office of Student Achievement, there are twenty-three "chronically failing schools" in the Atlanta Public School District.[29] In 2015, graduation rates for Black and Latinx students attending Atlanta Public Schools were 57 percent and 53 percent, respectively, while 84 percent of White students and 94 percent of Asian students graduated. It is no coincidence that Atlanta's failing schools are in some of the city's poorest neighborhoods, where economic mobility is the lowest, crime is high, gentrification is knocking on the door, and jobs are hard to find and hard to get to. However, some of the top universities in the world call Atlanta home, such as Spelman, Morehouse, Georgia Tech, and Georgia State University. Atlanta is not alone. With slight changes to a few percentages, you can apply this narrative to St. Louis; Baltimore; Detroit; Hartford, Connecticut; Washington,

DC; New Orleans; Dayton, Ohio; Kansas City, Kansas; and San Bernardino, California.

All these unflattering statistics about a city, which have everything to do with race and racism, leave dark folx criminalized, dehumanized, and disposable. They also leave communities without the resources and socioeconomic power to protect their children. A clear and sad example is the Atlanta Child Murders. From 1979 to 1981, twenty-nine or more Black boys and girls were kidnapped and killed. All of the victims came from low-income homes and some were in foster care. At the time, Atlanta was dealing with the backlash of the city's first Black mayor and a police department overwhelmed with racial tension and scandals.[30] I was protected because my gift was a high commodity according to American popular culture, and my community was performing right above stable, though slipping daily into what Rochester has now become. When communities sink into despair, girls and women are the most vulnerable. Because of sexism, misogyny, violence, and patriarchy, all women are vulnerable; however, dark girls are the most vulnerable, especially Black and Latinx girls, because they are criminalized both in the schools and in the streets. Monique Morris writes,

> Too many Black girls are being criminalized (and physically and mentally harmed) by the beliefs, policies, and actions that degrade and marginalize both their learning and their humanity, leading to conditions that push them out of school and render them vulnerable to even more harm.[31]

Morris is absolutely right: schools are pushing Black girls out of school into communities that are more equipped to harm them than to protect, nourish, and feed their gifts and potential. Atlanta's major sex trafficking industry preys on girls from toxic homes with high levels of poverty and brings in $290 million a year, more than illegal drug and gun trade combined.[32]

Dark communities are ill-equipped to protect girls of color. I was fortunate because I had a community and basketball. Black girls, as

I stated in chapter 2, are also expelled and suspended from school at high rates because teachers do not understand Black girls' struggles to live with dignity and stand up for themselves despite mental health issues, learning disabilities, and sexual and physical abuse. There is no amount of grit that can fight off the intersections of living in poverty, being pushed out of school, facing a world full of patriarchy and racism, and suffering toxic stress. It is not that dark children do not have grit and zest, but they need educators and their communities to protect it, not measure it. Sadly, this is easier said than done in an environment of injustice, profit from oppression, and quick fixes.

SYSTEM JUSTIFICATION

In June 2017, a study published in the journal *Child Development* found that youth of color from working-class families who grow up believing in America's narrative of hard work, perseverance, and grit—all components of character education—are more likely to participate in risky behavior and have lower self-esteem. The study is grounded in the social-psychological theory of "system justification," which explains how humans believe, defend, and rationalize the status quo because they see social, economic, and political systems as fair and legitimate. Among the low-income youth of color in the study, 91 percent believed in the "American dream." While holding system-justifying beliefs, these young people lacked the skills to interpret their world, which, sadly, is filled with intersectional, systemic oppression.

Erin Godfrey, the study's lead author, remarked on her team's findings in an article in the *Atlantic*: "We cannot equivocate when it comes to preparing our children to face injustices."[33] Godfrey's study confirms what Black, Brown, and Indigenous people have always known: "You cannot continue to oppress a consciously historical people."[34] Children of color attending schools that do not help them interpret the racist, sexist, Islamophobic, patriarchal, homophobic, transphobic, and xenophobic world in which they live is not only maintaining the status quo but also ensuring that Whiteness, patriarchy, and hate are never disrupted and challenged. Thus, White supremacy stays on track. There are folx who, no matter what you write about the grim plight of dark people or the brilliance and beauty of dark people, will believe in, defend, and uphold the system of White supremacy with every inch of their beings. Dark children's ugly circumstances are due to their deviant and lazy families, they explain, so grit and zest are necessary, and the children had better be thankful for it. The system always seems to win because Whiteness has the scorecard.

It took the system forty-six days for George Zimmerman to be arrested after he killed Trayvon Martin due to Florida's "stand your ground" law. Zimmerman told police that Trayvon attacked him and that he shot the teen in self-defense. On July 13, 2013, a year and a half after the shooting, Zimmerman was found not guilty of all charges for the death of Trayvon based on self-defense, or, more accurately, defense of the system (and defense of Whiteness).

As I finished this chapter, Mark texted me to reschedule; he had to visit his dad in rehab.

CHAPTER 5

ABOLITIONIST TEACHING, FREEDOM DREAMING, AND BLACK JOY

Let's begin by saying that we are living through a very dangerous time. Everyone in this room is in one way or another aware of that. We are in a revolutionary situation, no matter how unpopular that word has become in this country. . . . To any citizen of this country who figures himself as responsible—and particularly those of you who deal with the minds and hearts of young people—must be prepared to "go for broke." Or to put it another way, you must understand that in the attempt to correct so many generations of bad faith and cruelty, when it is operating not only in the classroom but in society, you will meet the most fantastic, the most brutal, and the most determined resistance. There is no point in pretending that this won't happen.

—JAMES BALDWIN[1]

EDUCATION CAN'T SAVE US. WE HAVE TO SAVE EDUCATION.

Abolitionist teaching is as much about tearing down old structures and ways of thinking as it is about forming new ideas, new forms of social interactions, new ways to be inclusive, new ways to discuss inequality and distribute wealth and resources, new ways to resist, new ways to agitate, new ways to maintain order and safety that abolishes prisons, US Immigration and Customs Enforcement, and mass incarceration, new ways to reach children trying to recover from the educational survival complex, new ways to show dark children they are loved in this world, and new ways to establish an educational system that works for everyone, especially those who are put at the edges of the classroom and society. Abolitionist teaching is teachers taking back their schools, classroom by classroom, student by student, parent by parent, and school community by school community. The work is hard and filled with struggle and setbacks, which is why Ella Baker's model of grassroots organizing rooted in creativity, imagination, healing, ingenuity, joy, and freedom dreaming is vital to the undoing of the educational survival complex and to all justice work.

Abolitionist teaching is not a teaching approach: It is a way of life, a way of seeing the world, and a way of taking action against injustice. It seeks to resist, agitate, and tear down the educational survival complex through teachers who work in solidarity with their schools' community to achieve incremental changes in their classrooms and schools for students in the present day, while simultaneously freedom dreaming and vigorously creating a vision for what schools will be when the educational survival complex is destroyed. No one teacher or parent can abolish the educational survival complex but if we work together, we can. Currently we are tweaking the system, knowing that these adjustments are what we need for the here and now, but we are always keeping our eyes on the root causes of dark children's suffering. Ella Baker once said that the "reduction of injustice is not the same as freedom."[2] The ultimate goal of abolitionist teaching is freedom. Freedom to create your reality, where uplifting humanity is at the center of all decisions. And, yes, concessions will be made along the way, battles will be lost, and sometimes teachers, parents, and community members will feel like they are not doing enough, but the fight is fought with the indomitable spirit of an abolitionist who engages in taking small and sometimes big risks in the fight for equal rights, liberties, and citizenship for dark children, their families, and their communities—this is fighting for freedom.

There is no one way to be an abolitionist teacher. Some teachers will create a homeplace for their students while teaching them with the highest expectations; some will protest in the streets; some will fight standardized testing; some will restore justice in their classrooms; some will create justice-centered curriculums and teaching approaches; some will stand with their students to end gun violence in schools; some will fight to end the prison-industrial complex in and outside of schools; some will fight in the effort so communities can peacefully govern themselves to control their children's education, housing, healthcare, and ideas about peace, justice, and incarceration; and some will do a combination of all of these. Still, some will leave the profession mentally, physically, and spiritually depleted, looking for a way to make an impact on education outside the classroom, but *all* are working to restore humanity with their eyes on abolishing the educational system as we know it. Abolitionist teaching is welcoming struggles, setbacks, and disagreements, because one understands the complexity of uprooting injustice but finds beauty in the struggle. Abolitionist teachers fight for children they will never meet or see, because they are visionaries. They fight for a world that has yet to be created and for children's dreams that have yet to be crushed by anti-Blackness.

TWEAKING THE SYSTEM IS NOT ENOUGH

For centuries, we have tried to tweak, adjust, and reform systems of injustice. These courageous efforts, righteous and just in their causes, are examples of the pursuit of freedom. However, we have learned from our collective freedom-building as dark folx that tugging at the system of injustice is just the first step, as White rage will counter and bring in reinforcements to maintain injustice. For example, when President Abraham Lincoln signed the Emancipation Proclamation on January 1, 1863, Texas slaveholders forced enslaved Black folx to remain in bondage for two and a half additional years. Black folx in Texas did not learn of their freedom until June 19, 1865, when Union soldiers arrived on the shores of Galveston, announcing the freeing of more than two hundred thousand enslaved Black folx in the state.

However, freedom was short-lived because the system and structures of oppressing dark people were not abolished at the root. The Thirteenth Amendment abolished slavery unless as a punishment for a crime. This deliberate, racist loophole forced free Black folx to become slaves all over again, as they were imprisoned for petty crimes such as vagrancy or were falsely arrested. They were returned to a new form of slavery for their alleged "crimes": the prison labor system or convict leasing. The South was accustomed to free Black labor and was not going to give that up because of a few laws or a Civil War; instead the system of slavery was able to be tweaked because its roots were still intact. Prisons sold the labor of Black men to local companies for cheap. While incarcerated and forced to work for pennies, these men also faced high fines and court fees for their petty crimes, if there was a crime at all. To pay back these "fees," prisoners were forced to work on plantations for "former" slaveholders, now known as prison holders. The bones of this unfair prisoner payment system are still in place centuries later. In 2016, over half a million people were in jail because they could not afford bail.[3] In the same year, eight hundred people died awaiting trial or serving short stints in jail for minor offenses.[4]

The work done in the fields was still done by dark bodies long after the Emancipation Proclamation was signed. The debt peonage system, or debt slavery, which was created from the centuries-old, established system of slavery, forced a person with no money, such as a newly freed slave, to agree to work on a plantation as a sharecropper. The landowner provided a portion of his land to use and the materials needed to farm; in return, the sharecropper gave a percentage of his earnings from the crops to the owner. The catch was that the prices of the supplies and land usage fees were so high that the sharecropper would never be able to pay off his debt. As a result, sharecroppers were in debt year after year, and the landowners remained their masters, even with slavery abolished on the books.

Folx who fight for prison abolition, such as Angela Y. Davis and Ruth Wilson Gilmore, understand that they are trying to tear down the prison-industrial complex while simultaneously building up radically revolutionary and sustainably empowering new systems of justice. History tells them, and us, that if we just change, adjust, or even eradicate one piece of the oppressive hydra, such as the prison-industrial complex or educational survival complex, another piece will grow in its place. They also understand the connection between the proliferation of prisons and other institutions in our society, such as public education. Reflecting on her work, Davis said in 2005, "Prison abolitionist strategies reflect an understanding of the connections between institutions that we usually think about as disparate and disconnected. They reflect an understanding of the extent to which the overuse of imprisonment is a consequence of eroding educational opportunities, which are further diminished by using imprisonment as a false solution for poor public education."[5] An ahistorical understanding of oppression leads folx to believe that quick fixes to the system, such as more surveillance, more testing, and more punishment, will solve the issues of injustice and inequality. This way of thinking is a fallacy of justice like the achievement gap is a fallacy of educational improvement.

ACHIEVEMENT GAP (SHARECROPPING)

The achievement gap is not about White students outperforming dark students; it is about a history of injustice and oppression. It is about the "education debt" that has accumulated over time due to the educational survival complex. It is one of the fallacies of justice to know that the achievement gap is due to race and class and yet never proclaim racism and White rage as the source of the achievement gap. Calling for teaching practices that tweak the system and for more resources are fine places to start but they will never radically change the system of persistent inequality in education. Dark students and their families are sharecroppers, never able to make up the cost or close the gap because they are learning in a state of perpetual debt with no relief in sight. But dark people still fight, hope, love, believe, and freedom-dream despite obstacles prepacked and tightly wrapped in racism, hate, and rage.

It is with this endurance that abolitionist teaching starts in the imagination of educators, but only after a deep and honest interrogation of America's antidarkness, racism, and White rage that created the educational survival complex. That imagination informs what is possible, as students and teachers are constantly told what is not possible in education, especially for dark children. New teachers walk into classrooms believing that inner-city schools cannot have a strong community, caring parents, and brilliant dark children. But my entire life is possible because dark folx freedom-dreamed. These dreams were filled with joy, resistance, love, and an unwavering imagining of what is possible when dark folx matter and live to thrive rather than survive. These freedom dreams and the places that helped them move into reality are important markers of what is possible.

BEACON HILL

There are two places in the US where I feel most alive, where my feet are on fire, my mind cannot stop racing, my soul feels whole, and my heart is filled with joy: Boston and New Orleans. To me, certain parts of these two cities embody abolitionist teaching: in New Orleans, it is Congo Square; in Boston, it is Beacon Hill. On the north side of Boston, in view of the Charles River and enclosed by Bowdoin Street, Cambridge Street, Boston Common, and Embankment Road, stands Beacon Hill. During the late 1700s through the mid-1800s, Beacon Hill was a well-established free Black community and the home of the abolitionist movement in the United States. Black and White abolitionists and newly freed Black folx from all over the country came to Beacon Hill to live, to work, to seek refuge, or to pass through one of its several Underground Railroad stops.

The Fifty-Fourth Massachusetts Infantry, the first Black soldiers allowed to fight in the Civil War, consisted of residents from Beacon Hill and throughout the US; fathers and sons enlisted together. Black men from all corners of the country came to Boston and Beacon Hill to serve in the Fifty-Fourth, including Charles and Lewis Douglass, sons of abolitionist Frederick Douglass. Governor John Andrew of Massachusetts, a member of the antislavery community, appointed Robert Gould Shaw to lead the all-Black infantry. Shaw initially declined but was persuaded by his parents, wealthy, well-connected White abolitionists. The free Black men of the Fifty-Fourth fought knowing that if they were captured they would be sold into slavery, and yet they refused their wages in protest because they were paid less than White soldiers. The Fifty-Fourth famously fought the battle of Fort Wagner, a Confederate stronghold. A glorious bronze memorial to these men currently resides at the edge of Boston Common across from the State House, the starting point of Boston's Black Heritage Trail.

Lewis and Harriet Hayden, two of the most radical and militant abolitionists of their time, lived on Beacon Hill. The Haydens' home was a safe house for newly self-emancipated Black folx and contained a secret tunnel for the Underground Railroad. Lewis was a member of the city's abolitionist Vigilance Committee and a recruiter for the Fifty-Fourth. The Vigilance Committee's job was to protect slaves from being captured and returned into slavery. It was well known that Lewis Hayden kept two kegs of gunpowder by the entryway of his home because he would rather have blown up his home than let a slave-catcher remove anyone from his property. The Haydens also provided shelter to the most famous of all enslaved runaways, Ellen and William Craft. Ellen, a biracial woman who could pass as White, and her husband, William, a Black man, were both born into slavery; however, in the winter of 1848, days before Christmas, they escaped their plantation in Macon, Georgia.

Ellen cut her hair and wrapped bandages around her face to hide her smooth skin. She wore men's trousers that she sewed herself. William was a skilled cabinetmaker who saved up enough money to pay for their travel north. The two left Macon on a train headed two hundred miles away to Savannah, Georgia. William rode in the "Negro car," while Ellen sat with the White folx pretending to be an elderly, deaf man so she would not have to talk to anyone. From Savannah, they boarded a steamboat to South Carolina, where a slaver trader offered to buy William from Ellen because William seemed so attentive to his "master." From South Carolina they went to Pennsylvania, a free state. Upon arrival in Philadelphia, they were taken in by abolitionists. Three weeks later, they moved to Beacon Hill, where William worked as a cabinetmaker and Ellen as a seamstress; they stayed with Lewis and Harriet Hayden for a time.

The Crafts became part of the abolitionist community in Boston, gave public lectures recounting their escape, and spoke out against slavery. William typically did most of the talking because women were not allowed to speak in a mixed-gender room. They lived in Boston for two years, then fled to England after slave-catchers arrived in Boston looking for them. They settled in West London, where they became public figures for the British abolitionist movement. After two decades of living overseas, the Crafts returned to Savannah to open a school for newly freed slaves.

White abolitionist William Lloyd Garrison, who encouraged the Crafts to tell their amazing story of bravery, intelligence, and determination, lived a few miles from Beacon Hill in Boston's Roxbury neighborhood. Garrison joined the abolitionist movement at the age of twenty-five. He published the antislavery newspaper the *Liberator*, which ran for thirty-five years and 1,820 issues. In the paper's first issue, Garrison wrote, "I do not wish to think, or speak, or write, with moderation. . . . I am in earnest—I will not equivocate—I will not excuse—I will not retreat a single inch—AND I WILL BE HEARD."[6] While jailed in Baltimore for his abolitionist work, he said, "A few White victims must be sacrificed to open the eyes of this nation."[7] Garrison also believed women should have the right to vote and was a supporter of the women's suffrage movement. He was a good friend of abolitionist Lucretia Mott, a White woman who was a powerful orator and one of the founders of the Philadelphia Female Anti-Slavery Society. Mott worked side by side with Elizabeth Cady Stanton and Susan B. Anthony, who led the women's suffrage movement. However, the movement was polluted with racism. Stanton and Anthony proclaimed that White women deserved the vote before Black women. Stanton once said, "We educated, virtuous White women are more worthy of the vote."[8] The fight for justice has to be intersectional. Stanton and Anthony were champions of women's rights but only those of White women. Mott, however, envisioned women's rights as an extension of human rights and the universal principles of liberty and equality.[9]

Beacon Hill is also home to the African Meeting House. Built in 1806, it was where abolitionists would gather to share ideas, strategies, and give powerful, memorable speeches that would shape America forever. The African Meeting House was also a recruitment site for the Fifty-Fourth Massachusetts Infantry. Funds needed to build the Meeting House were donated by Blacks and Whites. Frederick Douglass, William Lloyd Garrison, and Maria Stewart—who in 1833 became the first American-born woman to speak to a mixed-gender and mixed-race audience and who lived on Beacon Hill with her husband—all delivered their historic speeches at the African Meeting House. Born in 1803, nineteen years before Harriet Tubman and six years after Sojourner Truth, Stewart was a pioneer of Black feminism. She published her writings in the *Liberator*, which, like her speeches, called for women's rights, committing one's self to a life of activism, and creating Black-owned businesses.

Henry "Box" Brown spoke at the 1849 New England antislavery convention held in Boston. He was given the nickname "Box" because he escaped slavery by shipping himself from Virginia to Philadelphia in a wooden box, three feet long and two feet wide. Brown stayed still for twenty-seven hours, from wagon to train to steamboat to wagon again, until he reached freedom. Brown wrote in his book *Narrative of the Life of Henry Box Brown*, "If you have never been deprived of your liberty, as I was, you cannot realize the power of that hope of freedom, which was to me indeed, an anchor to the soul both sure and steadfast."[10]

Beacon Hill was also home to the Portia School of Law, at the time the only American law school for women. Blanche Woodson Braxton graduated from Portia (1921) and went on to become the first Black woman admitted to the Massachusetts bar and later the first Black woman to practice in a US district court. Mary Eliza Mahoney also lived on Beacon Hill and was the first Black female registered nurse. Josephine St. Pierre Ruffin, a resident of Beacon Hill and a Black woman, was the editor and publisher of the *Woman's Era*, the journal of the New Era Club, and she organized the national conference of the National Federation of Afro-American Women. Josephine's husband was Boston's first Black municipal judge. For a time, Phillis Wheatley, the first Black woman to publish a book of poetry in the US, also resided on Beacon Hill.

So many astonishing Black and White women and men from Beacon Hill and the surrounding area of Boston dedicated their lives to antislavery work, antiracism, and women's rights. They also fought for the right to educate Black children with dignity and humanity. In the late 1700s, Black Bostonians petitioned the state legislature, arguing that it was unfair for their taxes to pay for the education of White children while the city had no public schools for Black children. In 1798, sixty members of the Black community created the African School to educate their children. When the African Meeting House opened in 1806, the African School relocated there. When White businessman Abiel Smith died, he left $4,000 for the education of Black children. Parents used that money to build the Abiel Smith School in 1835 on Beacon Hill. The conditions of the Abiel Smith School were not comparable to those at the schools White children in Boston attended, so Black parents and coconspirators kept fighting. Many Black parents withdrew their children from the school in protest. These parents were quite aware of the educational survival complex for Black children even in the 1700s and 1800s.

In 1855, after decades of activism by Black parents, the Massachusetts legislature outlawed "separate schools." The first integrated school in Boston was the Phillips School on Beacon Hill, which at the time was considered one of the best schools in the city for White children. Once it was integrated, Elizabeth Smith, daughter of abolitionist John J. Smith, taught at the Phillips School. She is recorded as the first Black person to teach in Boston's integrated school system.

Beacon Hill is an example of what people can do when the ideas of abolitionism turn into a way of life; a way of seeing the world that does not normalize hate, White rage, and the inferior conditions for dark people; a way of life that relentlessly pursues and protects Blacks thriving. Beacon Hill also demonstrates that you do not have to be Black to be an abolitionist. Some abolitionists promoted militant action, such as Black abolitionist Nat Turner and White abolitionist John Brown. Some advocated for nonviolence, some wrote books and gave speeches that railed against slavery and injustice, some raised funds, some gave money, some taught, some fought in the war, some sued the government for equal rights under the law, some were healers, some community-organized, but all believed in the equality of Blacks and Whites and the tearing down of slavery, and believed in taking risks for those beliefs. Beacon Hill is a model for what is possible and for what abolitionist work is and can be in today's world of racism, sexism, hate, and rage. The people of Beacon Hill mattered to themselves and refused to live lives of mere survival. Their creativity, visionary thinking, boldness, collectivism, solidarity, and rebellious spirit form a vision for abolitionist teaching. We need Beacon Hills established throughout the country right now—spaces that not only protect those who are most vulnerable but also heal them. Beacon Hill's streets, buildings, and homes were filled with people who were accountable for one another's survival, spirit, education, and dreams of one day thriving. Beacon Hill is a model for dismantling the educational survival complex because it was powered by people fighting for their children and their children's children to matter.

CONGO SQUARE

As mentioned above, there is one more place on American soil where I feel the creativity, imagination, and ingenuity of free and enslaved dark folx who created art for Black joy with the beauty, love, and sophistication of darkness: Congo Square in New Orleans. Congo Square is a plot of land on North Rampart Street between St. Ann and St. Peter streets, currently nestled inside a park named after the great jazz musician Louis Armstrong. The park is located in the oldest Black community in New Orleans, Tremé.

Before Louis Armstrong ever blew his trumpet or the first notes of jazz were composed, there was Congo Square. For more than a century starting in the mid-1700s, enslaved Africans, free Blacks, and Native Americans were allowed to gather under the French *code noir*, which permitted worship and the selling of goods by enslaved human beings, but only on the Sabbath. Before the French arrived, the land was home to the Houmas Indians. On Sundays, festivals were organized around African and Afro-Caribbean dances, drums, songs, and the trading of goods. Enslaved Africans gathered, as many as six hundred on any given Sunday, to remember, to recall, and to honor what they were told and what they were forced to forget. What was created at Congo Square was the blending of sounds from Africa, the Caribbean, and Europe to form African American cultural expressions such as jazz, scatting, and swing. The rhythmic motifs, polyrhythmic sophistication, and complex, free-form yet structured improvisations of African music—combined with European instruments like the trumpet, bass, and snare drums—marked the sonic start of jazz. Arguably, there would be no jazz music without these incredible weekly gatherings at Congo Square.

But Congo Square is more than music; it's where personal and communal healing happened, where Black joy was found, and where resistance could be expressed in art. Social change cannot happen without art for joy and resistance. At Congo Square, enslaved Africans, Native Americans, and free Black folx shared the joy of their cultures, if only for a day. Even if they knew pain would follow on Monday morning, on Sundays they were using joy, love, and creativity as radical tools for Black expression and healing. Congo Square was a place to heal, recharge, and freedom-dream. They danced and sang together in a space cultivated by their cultures and they refused to let go. Education researcher and Black feminist Cynthia Dillard reminds us, "All too often, we have been seduced into forgetting (or have chosen to do so), given the weight and power of our memories and the often radical act of (re)membering in our present lives and work, that is (re)membering as an act of decolonization."[11] Abolitionist teaching is dependent on spaces like Congo Square to create art for resistance, art for (re)membering, art for joy, art for love, art for healing, and art for humanity.

ART

Writing, drawing, acting, painting, composing, spittin' rhymes, and/or dancing is love, joy, and resistance personified. Art provides more to communities than just visual and sonic motifs: it is one of the key ingredients to a better world. Art that inspires for a better world is rooted in intense design, research, and musings for justice filled with new-world possibilities. Social justice movements move people because they ignite the spirit of freedom, justice, love, and joy in all who engage with the work. Art helps people remember their dreams, hopes, and desires for a new world. Art is how people connect to what has been lost and what has not happened yet. Tom Feelings, author of the book *The Middle Passage: White Ships/Black Cargo*, said it best when speaking of the need for creativity by dark people:

> For four hundred years African creativity has been struggling to counter the narrow constraints of oppression, to circle it, turn it around, to seek order and meaning in the midst of chaos. My soul looks back in wonder at how African creativity has sustained us and how it still flows—seeking, searching for new ways to connect the ancient with the new, the young with the old, the unborn with the ancestors.[12]

Art education in schools is so important because, for many dark children, art is more than classes or a mode of expression; it is how dark children make sense of this unjust world and a way to sustain who they are, as they recall and (re)member in the mist of chaos what it means to thrive.

For many dark folx, art is a homeplace; art is where they find a voice that feels authentic and rooted in participatory democracy. Art can give this world hell. Art is a vital part of abolitionist teaching because it is a freeing space of creativity, which is essential to abolishing injustice. Writer and activist adrienne maree brown says, "All social justice work is science fiction. We are imagining a world free of injustice, a world that doesn't yet exist." Art first lets us see what is possible. It is our blueprint for the world we deserve and the world we are working toward. Abolitionist teaching is built on the radical imagination of collective memories of resistance, trauma, survival, love, joy, and cultural modes of expression and practices that push and expand the fundamental ideas of democracy. Art is freedom dreams turned into action because "politics is not separate from lived experience or the imaginary world."[13] The imaginary world creates new worlds that push democracy, which means politics, schooling, healthcare, citizenship, equal rights, housing, prison, and economics are reimagined for a just world.

Freedom dreaming is a relentless task for people on the margins of society; still, they create. They refuse to be invisible. Their art makes them visible and makes clear their intentions for love, peace, liberation, and joy. South African writer and Afrofuturist Lindokuhle Nkosi proclaims that "imagining yourself in the future is not revolutionary, it's survival."[14] I would add that creating from your imagination is not revolutionary or survival; it is moving toward thriving.

FREEDOM DREAMING

Abolitionist teaching starts with freedom dreaming, dreams grounded in a critique of injustice. These dreams are not whimsical, unattainable daydreams, they are critical and imaginative dreams of collective resistance. Robin D. G. Kelley, author of the book *Freedom Dreams: The Black Radical Imagination*, argues that a requirement for liberation as one refuses victim status is an "unleashing of the mind's most creative capacities, catalyzed by participation in struggles for change."[15] He goes on to write that "any revolution must begin with thought, with how we imagine a New World, with how we reconstruct our social and individual relationships, with unleashing our desire and unfolding a new future on the basis of love and creativity rather than rationality."[16]

The educational survival complex has become so rationalized and normalized that we are forced to believe, against our common sense, that inadequate school funding is normal, that there is nothing that can be done about school shootings, that racist teachers in the classrooms are better than no teachers in the classrooms. We have come to believe that police officers in our schools physically assaulting students is standard practice, and that the only way to measure a child's knowledge is through prepackaged high-stakes state tests, the results of which undermine teachers' autotomy, de-professionalize the teaching field, and leave dark children in the crosshairs of projected inferiority. After all the billions spent in test materials and meaningful teaching hours lost to test prep, dark children are held accountable for the failures of the public school system.

Dark children are retained, deemed academically malignant, and pushed out of schools with limited tools to survive. These dire situations call for freedom dreams of love for dark children and of a love for dark people's resiliency that is not glorified but is understood as a necessity in the face of White rage and in the fight for intersectional justice, solidarity, and a creativity that disrupts ideas we think are impossible. The great education philosopher and educator Maxine Greene once said, "To commit to imagining is to commit to looking beyond the given, beyond what appears to be unchangeable. It is a way of warding off the apathy and the feelings of futility that are the greatest obstacles to any sort of learning and, surely, to education for freedom. . . . We need imagination."[17] Arguably, abolitionists' greatest tools against injustice were their imaginations. Their imaginations fueled their resistance. Imagining being free, imagining reading, imagining marrying the love of your life, imagining your children being free, imagining life and not death, imagining seeing the world, and imagining freedom. These freedom dreams drive out apathy, and the quest for freedom becomes an internal desire necessary to preserve humanity.[18]

Freedom dreaming gives teachers a collective space to methodically tear down the educational survival complex and collectively rebuild a school system that truly loves all children and sees schools as children's homeplaces, where students are encouraged to give this world hell. This is why deep study and personal reflection on the history of the US is so important to abolitionist teaching. When an educator deeply understands why meaningful, long-term, and sustainable change is so hard to achieve in education because of all the forces antithetical to justice, love, and equity—such as racism, sexism, housing discrimination, state-sanctioned violence toward dark people, police brutality, segregation, hate-filled immigration policies, Islamophobia, school closings, the school-to-prison pipeline, and the prison-industrial complex—that is when freedom dreaming begins.

Understanding the mechanisms that reproduce structural inequality is an essential component of freedom dreaming. We cannot create a new educational system for all with a lack of understanding of what cripples our current system. Personally and collectively, freedom dreaming for intersectional social justice is what movements are made of; they start off as freedom dreams molded by resistance, self-determination, and struggle. Freedom dreaming is imagining worlds that are just, representing people's full humanity, centering people left on the edges, thriving in solidarity with folx from different identities who have struggled together for justice, and knowing that dreams are just around the corner with the might of people power. The marketplace will attack and attempt to co-opt these freedom dreams. Dreams will not be met because we ask, and they will be masked by corporate America's obsession with greed and attaching products to dark bodies and the justice work of dark bodies. Before I lay out the "work" of abolitionist teaching in detail, I think it is important to show how the fight for freedom is co-opted by culture vultures and corporate America for profit.

WATCH OUT FOR TAKERS

Case in point: Kendall Jenner's Pepsi commercial. In April 2017, an advertisement for the soda depicted people from all walks of life—though it explicitly highlighted dark bodies, especially those who are Muslim and queer—protesting, using their art for resistance, and dancing in the streets to the uplifting ballad "Lions" by Skip Marley, grandson of Bob Marley. The song is a call for unity. Marley sings, "We are the movement, this generation." As folx take to the streets to march for freedom, Jenner watches from her upscale photo shoot. In the most dramatic and contrived way possible, Jenner removes her wig, wipes off her lipstick, and joins the crowd after a handsome dark male gives her the okay. She is then the center of attention in a sea of dark bodies, in awe of what she is witnessing. While moving through the crowd, she grabs a conveniently placed Pepsi, fist-bumps a dark man, and the sound of a can of soda opening overpowers the music. Jenner walks up to one of the police officers working at the march and hands him a Pepsi. He drinks it, and the crowd goes wild. In short, Jenner unifies the cops and the dark bodies with a can of Pepsi.

Jenner is not known for her activism or for speaking out against injustice; she and her family have made millions profiting off Black culture. This commercial is just another attempt to squeeze dark people's freedom dreams for profit and is the perfect example of how social movements and freedom dreams get co-opted and reduced to gimmicks that make the masses feel good but do not result in any real change for justice. I highlight this commercial to illustrate how seductive corporate America can be in its attempts to water down social justice and center Whiteness. This Pepsi commercial is no different from movies that depict magical White teachers who save dark children from their "troubled" school and community, or teaching practices that center Whiteness, but never address racism. Again, profiting from the narrative that dark children need Whiteness and the gimmicks of the educational survival complex.

THE WORK

Abolitionist teaching moves beyond gimmicks and quick fixes to examine the root causes of the educational survival complex, teaches from a place of love and sharp criticism of the United States of America and antidarkness abroad, and activism. Examples of abolitionist teaching can be found all over the country: in 1998, the Tucson (Arizona) Unified School District began offering Mexican American history, literature, and art classes after community activists demanded that the school district reduce the number of students being pushed out of school. Not surprisingly, the ethnic studies classes drastically increased attendance, and students who took them reported higher graduation rates and college enrollment than students who were not enrolled in ethnic studies classes. In 2010, the state of Arizona banned ethnic studies classes focused on Mexican American history because state officials and school board members argued that the classes advocated resentment toward White people, even though the classes were open to all students and simply created "ethnic solidarity," as if ethnic solidarity were a bad thing. Students, parents, and teachers joined together in a fight to keep the classes that they knew were instrumental not only to the academic success of Chicano and Latinx students but also that taught them how beautiful their culture is and how their culture is an aspect of their lives that shows them they matter. Students in the Mexican American studies classes recited the poem "In Lak'ech: You Are My Other Me," by playwright Luis Valdez, the father of Chicano theater. The poem is based on the philosophical teachings of the ancient Mayans concerning empathy and integrity:

> *Si te amo y respeto,*
> *If I love and respect you,*
> *Me amo y respeto yo.*
> *I love and respect myself.*

This poem is an example of using students' culture to show them how they matter to themselves, their community, and the world. Ethnic studies classes can be students' homeplace. When the classes were banned, ethnic studies teachers, alumni of the program, and current students organized a grassroots movement led by youth with a participatory democracy model to fight to restore not only their classes but their humanity, because "a truthful, equitable and culturally appropriate education is understood to be a basic human right and not only a condition of Black people's individual success and collective survival. It is also fundamental to civilization and human freedom."[19] After ten years of fighting, in the summer of 2017, a federal judge ruled that banning the ethnic studies classes violated students' constitutional rights. The judge said that the ban's "enactment and enforcement were motivated by racial animus."[20] This is what abolitionism looks like in education.

In Seattle in 2013, teachers at a local high school voted unanimously to refuse to administer the MAP (Measure of Academic Progress) test. After the teachers refused to back down, and with parents and students standing in solidarity, it was ruled that the

MAP test would no longer be required in all high schools. In 2015, Seattle teachers went on strike to demand pay increases, which they deserved, but they also demanded and won thirty minutes of daily recess in all elementary schools; committees to examine equity issues across thirty schools, including investigating disciplinary measures that disproportionately affected dark children; a yearlong ban on out-of-school suspensions for elementary students; an end to using student standardized testing scores to evaluate teachers; the inclusion of teachers in decisions on the amount of standardized testing to be used; fewer students per special education teacher; and caseload limits for psychologists, occupational therapists, and other school-site specialists.

One central focus of the strike was to bring attention to the issues of equity centered on race and discipline within the district. Matt Carter, a special education teacher, addressed this issue head-on:

> I've spent my entire 14 years in Seattle working in southeast schools. When I look at the discipline numbers—the number of kids suspended and expelled—it's almost all African-American young men. Then you look at the rates up north, and if there are some, it's the few kids of color up there. It's so egregious and so obvious.
>
> We've asked for an equity team in every school. They told us it was a great idea, but they only want to do it in 6 schools out of 97 schools in the district. We absolutely said no. There are equity problems in every single school.[21]

Many parents supported the teacher strike. Naomi Wilson, a parent in the district, said, "Cost of living is definitely something that we support for teachers . . . but things like recess and reasonable testing and workloads and special education and equity—that's them fighting for us. Those are the issues we raised. So we come out strong and support their ability to bargain and fight not just for us, but for the education system. These are our kids. These are *my* kids."[22] After five days, the strike was over and teachers had received many of their demands. Of course, Seattle's schools are not now perfect beacons of equity, but teachers and parents found the power of their voices, grassroots organization, a politics of refusal, self-determination, and solidarity. At the end of the 2018 school year, the Seattle Education Association, which calls itself "the voice of Seattle public school educators," voted on a resolution calling for a moratorium on all standardized testing.[23] The efforts of Seattle's teachers are also an example of the meticulous, piece-by-piece tearing down of a system of injustice.

In 2018, there were teacher strikes in West Virginia, Kentucky, North Carolina, Colorado, Oklahoma, and Arizona calling for greater pay. Teacher pay in the US is down 5 percent, while class sizes are up and the cost of living is rising steeply.[24] Economic frustrations breed resistance, movements for justice, and solidarity. With the price of food and gas steadily increasing, high student loan debt, and low teacher pay, teachers could qualify for free and reduced lunch along with their students. Though I am being facetious, these conditions are forcing many teachers into debt, especially dark teachers, whose families were never allowed to buy into the American dream. I therefore support teacher strikes; however, we need to be critical of strikes that are not centered around issues of equity and race, because history tells us that dark people will always get the short end of the deal.

In September 2017, over 1,100 students in Denver, Colorado, walked out of school in protest of the Trump administration's decision to rescind Deferred Action for Childhood Arrivals (DACA). A month later, Dreamers blocked the vehicle entrance to Disneyland, chanting, "No dream! No deal!" This is the creativity and the people power needed, fueled by youth for the abolishment of injustice. United We Dream is an immigrant-youth-led national grassroots organization that Ella Baker would have been proud of. United We Dream has been organizing across the US under the vision:

> With a driving force of more than 400,000 members and an online reach of over 4,000,000 across the nation, we envision a society based on human dignity that celebrates all of our communities. We

understand that, in order to achieve this vision, how we do work must be reflective of the kind of society we aim to create: multi-ethnic, interdependent, intersectional, and inter-generational, all connected and reliant upon one another to achieve the highest standards for our collective humanity and liberation.

We embrace the common struggle of all people of color and stand up against racism, colonialism, colorism, and xenophobia. We stand against sexism, misogyny, and male-centered leadership while uplifting women leaders and the leadership of LGBTQ people. We work to make our spaces accessible to people of all abilities and seek to stand in solidarity and partnership with all who share our values.[25]

United We Dream's vision statement is an example of intersectional social justice and giving this world hell. This organization is freedom dreaming in real time. They understand that their humanity is entangled with everyone's humanity; the same for their citizenship. History has taught us that as long as one dark group's citizenship is in jeopardy, every dark group's citizenship is in jeopardy. United We Dream's vision is grounded in a collective struggle for humanity for all of us, not just undocumented youth. They are refusing to be silent, knowing that one of the most powerful tools they have against injustice is their voices. Their grassroots organizing, self-determination, and quest for human rights is teaching the world what is possible in the US. They are an exemplar of abolitionist teaching.

In January 2018, a letter from a third grader, King Johnson, gave this world hell when it went viral. King wrote a letter to his White teacher in his class journal asking her to stop teaching him lies about Christopher Columbus. King informed his teacher that he could not listen when he heard lies. He ends his journal entry by asking a question that has plagued the field of education since schools were disingenuously integrated: "How can White people teach Black history?"[26] Another exemplar of giving this world hell, self-determination, and the creativity of needed change is eleven-year-old Marley Dias, who started a book drive with the goal of collecting one thousand books that focus on girls of color. Her book drive, which gained international recognition, grew out of her frustration over and refusal to be exposed to books in school about "White boys and their dogs." There is also the boldness of Corrie Davis, a parent who fought the Cobb County, Georgia, school board and won after her son, who is Black, was called a slave by his White classmate on Civil War dress-up day. The White student came to school dressed as a plantation owner (slave owner). Cobb County schools will no longer have Civil War dress-up day. There are also teachers in solidarity with their students who are taking a knee during school events to protest police brutality and state-sanctioned violence.

A strong example of practicing a politics of refusal, visionary thinking, boldness, collectivism, and rebellion is seen with the students of Marjory Stoneman Douglas High School in Parkland, Florida. After a mass shooting at their school that killed fifteen of their classmates and two school officials, these students organized and inspired school walkouts across Florida and the US to protest gun violence in schools and call for gun reform or the banning of guns altogether. The young people from Parkland also led a national school walkout in March 2018. In a memorable and roaring speech aimed at politicians, Emma Gonzalez, a high school senior who survived the shooting and became one of the leading voices against the NRA and politicians who take the NRA's money, said, "We keep telling them that if they accept this blood money, they are against the children. . . . You're either funding the killers, or you're standing with the children. The children who have no money. We don't have jobs, so we can't pay for your campaign. We would hope that you have the decent morality to support us at this point."[27] David Hogg, Emma's classmate, asked politicians, "If you can't get elected without taking money from child murderers, why are you running?"[28] The courage of these young people as they attempt to radically change gun laws in the US is the courage and freedom dreaming of abolitionists.

Before the Parkland youth made national headlines with their activism, organizations such as Black Youth Project 100 and the Dream Defenders had been fighting gun violence for years. These groups' platforms push for an end to gun violence not just in our schools but in our communities. Black Youth Project 100 is the brainchild of political scientist Dr. Cathy Cohen. The organization focuses on developing members eighteen to thirty-five years old through a participatory democracy model that centers a Black queer feminist lens. Black Youth Project 100's "Agenda to Build Black Futures" calls for "shifts in economic policy in order to acquire the resources needed to build healthy lives, strong families, and communities."[29] Black Youth Project 100 has chapters throughout the US. Dream Defenders is a Florida-based organization, established in 2012, that declared, "In 2018, we were killed in our classrooms and on street corners. We were locked inside Florida's prisons and the keys were thrown away. We live in a state with more billionaires than almost anywhere in the country, yet, our parents and our teachers didn't have the basic resources they needed to keep us safe."[30]

As I stand with the youth of Parkland, I am reminded of how anti-Blackness works. The youth of Parkland were given a national microphone not only to discuss the loss of their classmates and their trauma but to speak out against gun violence and add to the intentionally elusive conversation on gun control in this country. Celebrities gave hefty financial contributions to support the efforts of the Parkland students' demonstration in Washington, DC, March for Our Lives, a movement to advance gun control. Dark organizations have been fighting for years on the issue of gun violence, inside and outside of schools. America's anti-Black attention span can focus on calling out and selling Black-on-Black crime for TV ratings, but it never focuses on Black folx' solutions to make their communities safe. This disparity is another reason why intersectional social justice is needed, so we can be inclusive but understand how anti-Blackness shifts the conversation and resources.

In February 2018, educators and parents from around the US organized around a national "Black Lives Matter Week of Action in Our Schools." The freedom dreaming started in 2016 in schools around the country. Two years later, schools in Seattle, Philadelphia, Rochester, Chicago, Boston, Baltimore, and DC taught children the struggle of Black people in all its beauty. The Prince George's County (Maryland) school board in 2018 passed a resolution called "Black Lives Matter Week of Action in Schools," which outlined how students will learn about and discuss not only the Black Lives Matter movement but how racism and discrimination function in society. The resolution states the following:

PRINCE GEORGE' S COUNTY BOARD OF EDUCATION

RESOLUTION

RESOLUTION REGARDING BLACK LIVES MATTER AT SCHOOL

WHEREAS, a national movement has arisen to assert that Black Lives Matter;

WHEREAS, this movement has raised awareness about injustices that exist at the intersections of race, class, and gender; including mass incarceration, police brutality, poverty, unaffordable housing, income disparity, homophobia, unjust immigration policies, gender inequality, and poor access to healthcare;

WHEREAS, in support of a national movement of teachers, parents, scholars and administrators who have come together to proclaim a week of action, affirmation, and solidarity, to be called "Black Lives Matter Week of Action in Schools";

WHEREAS, the thirteen guiding principles of the Black Lives Matter movement highlighted during this week of action are a means of challenging the insidious legacy of institutionalized racism and oppression that has plagued the United States since its founding;

WHEREAS, the purpose of the week will be to spark an ongoing movement of critical reflection and honest conversations in school communities for people of all ages to engage with critical issues of social justice . . .[31]

The intentionality of these words demonstrates these educators' deep sense of understanding how structural inequality is reproduced and how education that does not hide the truth from students is one of the first steps of freedom dreaming and fighting for freedom. The thirteen guiding principles of the Black Lives Matter movement highlighted in the resolution speak to the intersectional justice of Black Lives Matter: Black families, Black villages, Black women, collective value, diversity, empathy, globalism, intergenerationalism, love engagement, queer affirmation, restorative justice, transgender affirmation, and being unapologetically Black.[32] These principles affirm inclusiveness but center those at the margins of society. The push for justice by students, parents, and community members cannot be done without solidarity and a reflectiveness of self.

Teachers from around the country are forming organizations to freedom-dream new teaching methods, classrooms, community partnerships, and school systems built with intersectional social justice at the roots of their foundations. Badass Teachers Association, New York Collective of Radical Teachers, Caucus of Working Educators, Teacher Action Group in Philadelphia and Boston, Teachers of Social Justice in Chicago, Teachers 4 Social Justice in San Francisco, Black Teacher Project, Institute for Teachers of Color Committed to Racial Justice, Educators' Network of Social Justice in Milwaukee, Education for Liberation Network, Association of Raza Educators in San Diego and Oakland, and Free Minds, Free People are all teacher-activist organizations that will move us forward in tearing down the educational survival complex and creating an education system thought by some to be impossible.[33]

In 2018 the Rochester City School District introduced an antiracism and cultural competency pedagogy that emphasizes building personal relationships with students and their families, called Victorious Minds Academy. One of the goals of VMA is to recognize how structural racism and White supremacy function "from classrooms, principals' offices, and the downtown headquarters."[34] VMA grew out of the work of Dr. Joy DeGruy, an expert on antiracism. Her book *Post Traumatic Slave Syndrome* is the driving force of VMA. The district worked closely with DeGruy to develop an academy for teachers that helps them recognize the lasting impact of the historical trauma of slavery on students of color, how culturally responsive teaching recognizes that students of color may learn differently from White students but does not see that as a deficit, and the importance of building relationships with both the child and the family rather than just sharing knowledge of and building on students' assets instead of pointing out their deficits.[35] Abolitionist teaching on a wide scale requires the willingness of teachers and school administrators to address systemic racism and its effects on dark children while loving Blackness enough to see its assets so that dark children matter.

There are many, but two abolitionist teachers I want to highlight are Jahana Hayes and Mandy Manning; both were awarded the prestigious title of National Teacher of the Year, in 2016 and 2018, respectively. Hayes left education to run for office as the state of Connecticut's first Black Democrat to serve. Hayes says she is running because, "I feel like I'm at a point in my life where I have a responsibility to speak up for my community. We need someone who will speak to what's happening in public education, what's happening on our borders, what's happening to our organized labor unions—because all these people who work every day and contribute in our community . . . feel like they're left out of the conversation."[36]

In 2018, when Manning arrived at the White House to officially be awarded National Teacher of the Year, she handed President Donald Trump a stack of letters from her students, who are refugee and immigrant children. She also staged a silent protest by wearing political pins that were highly visible to the president. One of her pins read "Trans Equality Now" and another was a rainbow-colored apple to support LGBTQ rights in education. In her application for Teacher of the Year, Manning wrote:

> In the current political climate, anti-immigrant and anti-refugee rhetoric is rampant. . . . As soon as my students arrive, they are afraid they will have to leave. Most of my students come to the U.S. seeking safety, but they don't always feel safe here. This makes

it hard for them to share and learn from others. I must help them understand current events, know their rights, and provide a safe and welcoming environment.[37]

Hayes and Manning are using their platforms to fight for intersectional justice and sound the alarm of the everyday realities dark children and their families endure, while trying to just survive.

Lastly, I want to discuss another remarkable place of freedom dreaming and abolitionist teachings outside of schools. Jackson, Mississippi, is a city pursuing freedom by building new democratic institutions that place power in the hands of the people. Through participatory democracy and a vision for economic solidarity, Jackson has become what Robin D. G. Kelley calls "America's most radical city, where a genuinely revolutionary movement is building our first cooperative commonwealth dedicated to the principles of democracy, human rights, workers' power, environmental sustainability, and socialism."[38] Black folx in Jackson and their coconspirators have embraced radical democratic traditions of abolition democracy. Kelley writes:

> This radical democratic tradition cannot be traced to the founding fathers or the Constitution or the Declaration of Independence. Instead, it is manifest in the struggles of the dispossessed to overturn the Eurocentric, elitist, patriarchal, and dehumanizing structures of racial capitalism and its liberal underpinnings. It is manifest in the struggle to restore the "commons" to the commonwealth, which has been at the heart of radical abolitionism—or what Du Bois called the Abolition Democracy.[39]

Jackson's vision is a vision of freedom, a vision of giving this country's government hell, a vision that will not be won without struggle. Chokwe Lumumba, a lawyer and freedom fighter, was elected mayor of Jackson in 2013. Lumumba was the leader of the New Afrikan People's Organization and the Malcolm X Grassroots Movement.

Lumumba moved to Jackson from Detroit in 1971 with the Provisional Government of the Republic of New Afrika (PGRNA), "a movement for Black self-determination that envisioned the South as the site for establishing an independent Black nation."[40] PGRNA bought land in Jackson, established cooperative farms, and freedom-dreamed a new vision of democracy grounded in the ideas of abolition democracy. Their vision is the foundation of Jackson's racial vision today. A year after being elected mayor, Chokwe Lumumba died, but his ideas did not. His son, Chokwe Antar Lumumba, ran for mayor and won in 2017. Of course, White rage is raging. The state government is trying to take local control away from the Black city council by introducing legislation that would relinquish control of the city's airport and commerce from the mayor's office and city council. The state also reallocated funds from the city's 1 percent sales tax aimed at infrastructure stability.[41] There will always be setbacks, missteps, pushback, and losses in the fight for justice. Whiteness is resisting too. Whiteness will counterpunch and try to knock you out because Whiteness is consumed by its self-interest. However, activism, no matter how big or how small, grounded in the teachings and dreams of abolitionist and participatory democracy, will win.

The ideas of Jackson, VMA, the New York Collective of Radical Teachers, the Dream Defenders, "Black Lives Matter Week of Action in Our Schools," the students of Marjory Stoneman Douglas High School, Marley Dias, King Johnson, the community that fought for the Tucson Unified School District's ethnic studies classes, United We Dream, and all the parents, teachers, students, artists, and activists—their struggles make freedom dreaming possible and abolitionist teaching a reality.

SOLIDARITY

On June 27, 2015, Bree Newsome strapped on her climbing gear, climbed a flagpole over South Carolina's State House, and removed its Confederate flag. It seemed liked a spontaneous act of rebellion, but it was calculated, well timed, and done in solidarity with others so that a Black woman would be the one who took down the flag. Nine days before Newsome's climb, White supremacist Dylann Roof entered the oldest African Methodist Episcopal Church in the South, affectionately called Mother Emanuel, sat with churchgoers during Bible study, then shot and killed nine people while yelling racial epithets at his victims. Days later, it was revealed that Roof had posted hateful, racist, and anti-Semitic messages online, including a picture of himself holding a handgun and a Confederate flag.

Newsome's removal of the Confederate flag was not just about protesting the flag and the hate and racism it incites. It was also about the victims and the survivors of the church shooting and racial injustice everywhere. As Newsome scaled the flagpole, authorities waited below to arrest her. However, they also had another plan to get her down: to tase the pole with their taser gun, which could have killed Newsome. Her coconspirator, James Tyson, a White man, also waited at the bottom, tightly hugging the pole so that if they tased the pole, they would tase him too. The two had met just days before they took down the flag. Both Newsome and Tyson were from Charlotte, North Carolina; both were seasoned activists; and both had been arrested during separate civil disobedience acts in Raleigh at an event called Moral Monday. Their paths crossed at a meeting in Charlotte at which local activists were planning to take down a Confederate flag. Newsome volunteered to climb a flagpole at South Carolina's State House, but she was not an experienced climber. She had to train. Newsome, Tyson, and another activist practiced climbing poles around Charlotte leading up to the South Carolina flag removal. The day of the removal, Newsome and Tyson waited in an IHOP parking lot in the wee hours of the morning for the signal to scale the pole. In an interview after the event, Tyson said, "We did have some support from deep-pocketed allies who bought the climbing gear and promised to cover bail."[42] At 6:15 a.m., they got the go-ahead text.

Newsome and Tyson made history that day and showed the world what is possible. These two strangers put their lives on the line for each other; they were willing to risk it all to symbolically remove racism. Beyond the symbolism of their efforts is an example of solidarity, trust, and the deliberate centering of a Black woman to be the face of justice. Tyson was more than her ally; he was her coconspirator.

COCONSPIRATORS, NOT ALLIES

In many intersectional social justice groups, the language is shifting from needing allies to coconspirators. Ally-ship is working toward something that is mutually beneficial and supportive to all parties involved. Allies do not have to love dark people, question their privilege, decenter their voice, build meaningful relationships with folx working in the struggle, take risks, or be in solidarity with others. They just have to show up and mark the box present; thus, ally-ship is performative or self-glorifying. This type of ally-ship still centers Whiteness in dark spaces. Too often, though not always, our allies are eager White folx who have not questioned their Whiteness, White supremacy, White emotions of guilt and shame, the craving for admiration, or the structures that maintain White power. Also, how can allies work from the mindset of mutuality if they are the dominant group? I have personally witnessed allies take over the conversation and make the meeting about their singular issue; they act as an authority on a community they have never lived in, and they stop freedom dreams because they are not interested in tearing down systems that benefit them and their loved ones but not the rest of us. They also do not know how to work their privilege for dark lives.

Tyson put his body on the line for Newsome understanding that his White skin and his gender were her protection. He knew the chances of the police killing a White man on camera in broad daylight would be far less than those of killing a Black woman by herself. His Whiteness was her protection. Tyson was not an ally; he was a coconspirator who understood how Whiteness works in our society. He was willing to use his intersections of privilege, leverage his power, and support Newsome to stand in solidarity and confront anti-Blackness. A coconspirator functions as a verb, not a noun.

Coconspirators can also be men who understand their privilege and work to challenge and undo patriarchy.

The backbone of abolitionist teaching is solidarity with courageous coconspirators. Coconspirators work toward and understand the following, according to Allies for Change, a network of educators and activists committed to sustained "life-giving ally relationship":

- Understanding where we stand in relation to systems of privilege and oppression, and unlearning the habits and practices that protect those systems, which is lifelong work for all of us, without exception
- Authentic relationships of solidarity and mutuality, which are not possible when we try to avoid or transcend power imbalances
- Honestly acknowledging and confronting those imbalances to create authentic relationships
- Social change work is always rooted in collaboration, humility, and accountability
- The interior journey into silence, mediation, inner wisdom, and deep joy is inextricably linked to the outer work of social change[43]

These steps are the internal work that needs to happen before the outside work can start. One cannot enter freedom-dreaming spaces holding on to dark people's nightmares. We cannot have conversations about racism without talking about Whiteness. The time-consuming and serious critique and reflection of one's sociocultural heritage—which includes identities related to race, ethnicity, family structure, sexuality, class, abilities, and religion—taken side by side with a critical analysis of racism, sexism, White supremacy, and Whiteness is the groundwork of coconspirators. It also presents time to challenge what you think about your own educational experiences and resources in relation to the issues your students and their communities face. It is time to reflect on your educational history that either enabled or prevented you from achieving. How do resources such as your family, school structure, curriculum, materials, school funding, and community support help you thrive in education? This type of deep personal reflection is a must before taking up space in spaces that are trying to build, heal, and tear down all at the same time while never forgetting that joy is central to the work of freedom.

Whitney Dow, creator of the Whiteness Project, captured the work best when he said, "Until you can recognize that you are living a racialized life and you're having racialized experiences every moment of every day, you can't actually engage people of other races around the idea of justice."[44] When speaking about White guilt, Dow adds, "I could do something inside and that would change things. It kind of eliminated guilt for me. It made me feel incredibly empowered and really enriched my world." Dow is describing the inner work that is needed when you are White and fighting for justice in solidarity with dark folx. Molly Tansey, coauthor of *Teaching While White* and a former student of mine, says that early on in her teaching career she was "driven by the self-satisfaction" of making it visible to her peers that she was not racist.[45] But the real work for Molly began when she started having conversations acknowledging her White privilege with other White people; when she began to name Whiteness and its privileges with her White friends, family members, and colleagues. This is the work of challenging Whiteness in your community so you can challenge it at school. The work is not a onetime conversation; it is who you must become in and outside the classroom.

BLACK JOY

The hashtags #BlackGirlMagic, #BlackBoyJoy, #BlackGirlsRock, #CareFreeBlackKids, #BlackManJoy, and #BlackJoyProject are not just social media gimmicks or trends; they are what is needed for resistance, freedom, healing, and joy. Joy is crucial for social change; joy is crucial for teaching. Finding joy in the midst of pain and trauma is the fight to be fully human. A revolutionary spirit that embraces joy, self-care, and love is moving toward wholeness. Acknowledging joy is to make yourself aware of your humanity, creativity, self-determination, power, and ability to love abundantly. Freedom dreams are brought to life through joy and love of dark people's light. Joy makes the quest for justice sustainable. Black feminist Brittney Cooper writes that joy "is critical in reinvigorating our capacity for a new vision. When we lack joy, we have diminished capacity for self-love and self-valuing and for empathy. If political struggle is exercise for the soul, joy is the endorphin rush such struggles bring."[46] We cannot freedom-dream without joy.

Abolitionists loved; abolitionists found joy in some of the most hideous conditions; abolitionists formed communities from the love and joy of people in search of their full humanity. Joy provides a type of nourishment that is needed to be dark and fully alive in White spaces, such as schools. Abolitionist teaching is not just about tearing down and building up but also about the joy necessary to be in solidarity with others, knowing that your struggle for freedom is constant but that there is beauty in the camaraderie of creating a just world.

There is joy and then there is Black joy. Both are necessary for justice; however, Black joy is often misunderstood. Black joy is to embrace your full humanity, as the world tells you that you are disposable and that you do not matter. Black joy is a celebration of taking back your identity as a person of color and signaling to the world that your darkness is what makes you strong and beautiful. Black joy is finding your homeplace and creating homeplaces for others. Black joy is understanding and recognizing that as a dark person you come with grit and zest because you come from survivors who pushed their bodies and minds to the limits for you to one day thrive.

Abolitionist teaching is not sustainable without joy. Dark students have to enter the classroom knowing that their full selves are celebrated. Not just their culture, language, sexuality, or current circumstances but their entire selves, past, present, and future. Their ancestors, their family members, their friends, their religion, their music, their dress, their language, the ways they express their gender and sexuality, and their communities must all be embraced and loved. Schools must support the fullness of dark life as a way to justice. Abolitionist teaching is searching for spaces of understanding and affirming. Abolitionists dreamed in full color of what life would be without oppression. Black joy makes that world manageable for dark people; it is how we cope. It is how we love. Black joy is not wishful thinking; it is a love for those who made it possible for you to stand tall and believe in tomorrow, because you have a blueprint of resistance, love, and strength in your DNA. Abolitionist teaching harnesses Black joy because it is Black joy. There are no grit lab tests for Black joy, and Black joy is infectious.

Teachers who understand Black joy enter the classroom knowing that dark students knowing their history, falling in love with their history, and finding their voice are more important than grades. Good grades do not equal joy. Black joy is knowing that you are more than your trauma while understanding that healing from trauma is a process.

White folx can also embrace Black joy by helping, advocating for, and wanting Black folx to win. Recognizing and acknowledging White privilege is cute, but what does it mean without action? Dismantling White privilege is giving something up so Black folx can win. If folx with privilege are not using their privilege to demand justice and advocate for dark folx and all their identities, then they are complicit in White rage or male rage and thus are condoning injustice, violence, and the educational survival complex. By winning, I mean White folx ensuring that people of color are being paid equally or more than their White peers. White teachers demanding that schools hire more teachers of color. Silencing your White voice so dark folx' voices can be heard. White folx bringing dark folx in on all decision-making and dark folx having equal or more weight, and not just on issues about injustice or education but on issues that impact all of us, regardless of the color of our skin. White folx embracing Black joy is loving seeing dark people win, thrive, honor their history, and be fully human.

ACCOUNTABILITY

Accountability is a word used in the field of education to scare educators into spirit-murdering dark children. Educators are held accountable for their students' academic achievements by mandated federal policies attached to school funding. Federal standard-based accountability intensified in 2001 with the passage of No Child Left Behind. In essence, NCLB was a federal surveillance system that monitored student achievement, accreditation of teacher-preparation programs, and teacher licensure. NCLB's oversight was framed as a way of "protecting the public from educational malpractice, or, more ambitiously, of ensuring that high standards are met."[47] Monitoring students' achievement on a federal level opened up the floodgates for corporate money to enter education. While companies were profiting from the narrative that they were protecting the public, we stopped protecting dark students' potential, if we ever had. And we stopped being accountable for the pain, hurt, trauma, and wrongdoings, if we ever had been. Abolitionist teaching asks us to be accountable for the pain we have caused others, to restore justice, and call into question our liberal politics. The great Audre Lorde said, "The true focus of revolutionary change is never merely the oppressive situations which we seek to escape, but that piece of the oppressor which is planted deep within each of us."[48] Abolitionist teaching asks us to question the piece of the oppressor that lives in all of us.

As educators, we need to think of accountability beyond testing and academic achievement, and in terms of human suffering. How do we hold teachers accountable for injustices in their classrooms that they themselves have caused? How do we hold men accountable for restoring justice due to the harm of patriarchy? How do we hold a country accountable for restoring justice after putting children in cages and causing irreversible levels of toxic stress? Abolitionist teachers have to hold themselves and their colleagues to a level of accountability that focuses on justice, love, healing, and restoring humanity. Educators, and especially those with privilege, must be responsible for making sure dark children and their families win.

Abolitionist teaching is asking a lot of all teachers, but any good pedagogy should. Any pedagogy that does not interrogate and challenge Whiteness is inadequate, especially since more than 80 percent of the teaching force is White. Any pedagogy that does not help teachers contextualize students' realities is inadequate because no student is solely responsible for their reality. And any pedagogy that does not challenge injustice is useless because survival is not the goal. Abolitionist teaching asks a lot because the work is too important not to. Our schools and our teaching practices do not need to be reimagined; they need to be torn down and replaced with our freedom dreams rooted in participatory democracy and intersectional justice.

CHAPTER 6

THEORY OVER GIMMICKS

Finding Your North Star

*I came to theory because I was hurting—the pain within
me was so intense that I could not go on living. I came to
theory desperate, wanting to comprehend—to grasp what
was happening around and within me. Most importantly,
I wanted to make the hurt go away. I saw in theory then a
location for healing.*

—BELL HOOKS[1]

BLAME GAME

It may seem odd or cruel to find joy and comfort after reading about
someone's pain, but when I first read the words above by bell hooks, I
smiled. I felt my emotions take a deep breath of relief. My body went
still and began to repair itself. I needed these words in my quest for
wholeness, not only as a dark person but as a human being wrestling
with a world that prides itself on being unrecognizable to humanity. I smiled because hooks, like she has done as a writer and critical
thinker for the past forty years, conveyed in written form what my
entire being had been trying to express for years but lacked the emotional and intellectual understandings to do so. I needed a way to pull
my thoughts and feelings together to say something that explained to
myself the world in which I lived.

School shootings. Families living out of their cars despite working
sixty hours a week. Cops shooting unarmed dark bodies with impunity. Teachers murdering the spirits of students. Families being tar-

geted and torn apart by hateful immigration policies. Mosques being burned to the ground. Black trans women being murdered and no one caring outside the Black queer community. CEOs making billions while their employees fight for a living wage. Hospitals dumping their patients onto the streets. Finding out your favorite actor is a sexual predator and a disgusting human being. Listening to callous updates on America's endless wars followed by bland news reports on our possible entrance into a new war. Our country's children walking out of schools to demand their own safety at school, what should be the simplest of requests. Athletes taking a knee during the national anthem to protest dark death. And Black lives still not mattering. These momentous events were all just blips in one twenty-four-hour news cycle of our humanity screaming for help. While it is almost too much for any one person to take, educators must digest these realities and more.

By more, I mean that abolitionist teachers must process and respond in some meaningful way to the lives of our students and their own lives as well. But how do we understand what we are experiencing all around us with our own biases, inundated with political sound bites that never truly explain anything regardless of political party, and centuries-old myths about children of color, their families, and their communities that get remixed for present-day forms of suffering? How do we make sense of it all without losing our minds, retreating from reality, giving up, and/or spirit-murdering children? When the world does not make sense, when we are desperate, yearning to comprehend and frantically needing to place blame for what we see, how do we make these decisions? How do our conclusions about who is to blame impact our teaching and interactions with our students and their families?

If some teachers believe that the system is just, that racism and sexism are only individually distributed and not systemic (if they exist at all), and that hard work is the only key ingredient to becoming whatever you want to be in life, then how do teachers make sense of poverty (e.g., intergenerational racial wealth disparities), failing schools, crime, violence, the prison-industrial complex, and health disparities?

TEACHER EDUCATION GAP

As a teacher at a predominantly White institution, I see that many of my undergraduate students have never had meaningful interactions with dark people. My students are mostly White, middle-class young women between the ages of eighteen and twenty-one, which is the demographic of most teacher education programs in the US. I even have students whose grandparents were in the KKK. The first, and only, time I had a number of dark students in one of my undergrad classes—five, to be exact—one of my dark students overheard a White classmate call another student's Black boyfriend a "nigger" at a party off-campus. In the spring of 2018, another student describing an Asian man in her paper called him "oriental." I had to explain that "oriental" describes a rug, not a person. A few years ago, a student wrote in one of her papers that traveling to South Africa was the first time she had been around African American students. I simply wrote on her paper, "See me after class." I wanted her to have a conversation with me and not just read my comments in the margins and move on. Worried about her grade, she came up to me right after she got her paper. I informed her that she was not interacting with African American people but with South Africans while she was in South Africa. I told her African Americans are right here in Georgia. I am one of them. You do not need to go across the world to find African Americans. Her face turned red. She was embarrassed and assured me that she knew the difference.

After our brief chat, I was clear about one thing: yes, she knew the difference, but her interactions with African Americans were limited and so much about our very existence was unknown to her and, really, to most of my students. I took this great teaching moment to explain to her and the class that you do not have to go across the world to interact with Black people or people of color, as a number of my students every year go on church mission trips to dark countries. My goal as an educator, teaching overwhelmingly White students, is to get White students to question how they are going to teach children of color with a limited understanding of who these children are, where these children come from, their history, why and how they matter to the world, who loves them, why they should love Blackness, why they should want to see dark children win, how to support their quest to thrive, and how it is intentional that future teachers know so little about dark students. And, most important, how did my White students come to know what they know about dark students. Students knowing so little about dark people is not an accident; racism erases dark bodies from historical records of importance and distorts their everyday reality.

To be clear, not only my students but students in teacher education programs everywhere and, sadly, in-service teachers from all over the country walk into classrooms with preconceived notions and stereotypes about dark children. Research has shown that teacher preparation programs have been largely ineffective in preparing White teachers to teach diverse student populations.[2] For that reason, I am a realist. One sixteen-week class with me will not drastically change my students' ideas of dark children, but it may, hopefully and importantly, interrupt them. I ask my students every year to guess the percentage of Black people in the US population. I am always blown away by this activity because their estimations are so high. Guesses range from 20 to 40 percent. In reality, Black folx make up just less than 14 percent of the US population. So, if you have limited interactions with Black folx, how can you think there are so many of us?[3] Again, Black folx are highly visible and invisible at the same time. The sad truth is that White people can spend their entire lives ignoring, dismissing, and forgetting dark peoples' existence and still be successful in life. The latter is not the same for us.

Teacher education programs also perpetuate the stereotyping and myth-making targeted at dark children and their communities. I call this the "Teacher Education Gap." For example, many education programs have one diversity course in which White students learn about all the ills that plague dark communities without any context of how Whiteness reproduces poverty, failing schools, high unemployment, school closings, and trauma for people of color. Future teachers learn that dark children are in trauma, dark children are "at-risk," dark children are "underprivileged," dark children fall into the achievement gap, and dark communities are underserved, living in poverty. But how did this reality happen, and is that all? Where is the beauty, the resistance, the joy, the art, the healing, redemption, and the humanity and ingenuity of people making something out of nothing? Just as important, where is the critique of the system that perpetuates injustice and dark suffering in and outside the walls of schools?

Few teacher education programs require their students to take classes in African studies, African American studies, Latinx studies, Caribbean studies, Chicana/o studies, American studies, and/or Native American studies. Teachers of all backgrounds walk into classrooms never studying the history or the culture of the children they are going to teach. So, how can teachers be culturally relevant when they have not studied culture? Culture does not simply fall from the sky. Traditions and ways of being are intentionally created and crafted because culture reflects the educational, social, economic, political, and spiritual conditions of people.

Culture is not as biological as we think. It is a group's knowledge production process that occurs as they understand and respond to their reality and create ways of being to survive or thrive in their everyday lives. Whiteness is also a culture; it was created by the educational, social, economic, spiritual, and political conditions that intentionally and methodically give power to racism. This is why Whiteness is so hard to remove from society. To abolish Whiteness means dismantling the structures that maintain its power and influence. If we, teacher educators, are going to ask teachers to be culturally relevant and culturally competent—which I wholeheartedly believe are fundamental to challenging inequities and develop critical perspectives—then teachers should be required to study culture.

If teachers studied and understood Black culture, per se, they would know that the culture is filled with self-expression, complex language shifting abilities, creativity, self-advocacy, focus play (i.e., hand clap games), memory, and improvisation. Let me stop here to say: Black folx improv not because we do not understand the structure, but because we know the structure so well. Improvisation is resistance. My point here is not to generalize Black people or paint us as monolithic, but to say that many of us have experienced similar educational, historical, social, economic, political, and spiritual conditions, so we share a culture. Teachers need to know the beauty of that culture, not just the hardships, that produces beautiful minds, many of which are sitting right in front of them. An entry from one of my master's students' reflection logs encapsulates this need to know more about Black culture when learning about culturally relevant pedagogy (CRP), dark students in general, and Whiteness. She wrote: "When Dr. Love asked us to describe black culture after reading about CRP, I was frozen. I realized that we as educators do need to know the specifics of what cultural differences look like (I had never considered this before), but also how fine the line is between stereotyping and describing culture. After class that day, I went out to lunch, and Jiwon (a Korean classmate) asked me to describe white culture, what it was like growing up white in Mississippi. I basically couldn't." My student's log illustrates the need for more robust conversations about culture, race, and learning styles. Without examining culture, educators will turn to stereotypes instead of rich examples that explain dark life and provide context to their lived realities.

STARBUCKS

Teacher education programs on the topics of racism, diversity, privilege, and intersectionality are just slightly better than Starbucks on the matter. After two Black men were arrested at a Starbucks store in Philadelphia in 2018 simply for sitting down, the company decided to close its stores nationwide for a half day of mandatory racial-bias training for its 175,000 employees. Several news outlets reported on employees' reactions after the training. A big takeaway was that Starbucks was asking its employees not to be color-blind but "color brave," a term coined by Mellody Hobson, a Black woman who is president of a Chicago-based investment firm with $12.4 million in assets and a board member of Starbucks. To be color brave means to speak openly and honestly about race.[4] Being color brave is a great idea on the surface, but what happens after those conversations or when the supposedly open and honest conversation is filled with hate, lies, and stereotypes about dark people, with no accountability for reconciliation? Starbucks' adding fancy terms, a high-quality short documentary on racial biases, celebrity cameos, and a few hours of training to address this country's four-hundred-year history of anti-Blackness is almost the equivalent of teacher education programs offering one class on diversity that highlights oppression but never explains it or implicates Whiteness. One Starbucks employee, Jason, a Black man, said after the training, "There were times where I felt like they missed the mark. . . . It seemed like a lot of talking from videos and not enough discussion from us."[5] An Arkansas-based employee, who remained anonymous, said, "While this may be the most cost-efficient way to handle the situation, I don't feel like it will change much of anything. . . . Just driving an hour down the road takes you to towns where racism is alive and well."[6]

Teacher education programs ask students to speak openly and honestly about race and racism without the students having any understanding about where they stand in relation to systems of privilege and oppression and how these systems function in their everyday lives. Whiteness "is a category of identity that is most useful when its very existence is denied."[7] The invisibility of Whiteness and its extensive history of violence make Whiteness a hard concept to grasp. Therefore, my hope is that my students' personal social justice journey of making Whiteness visible starts in my class, but it cannot end there. The misguided and episodic classes on diversity in teacher education exacerbate the educational survival complex. Teachers go into the field with limited understanding of the children they are teaching and how schools fail students, not the other way around, and therefore they believe we need more testing and zero-tolerance approaches, and that the system is just.

Another facet of the teacher education gap is White students' limited interactions with people of color, which perpetuates the myths about people of color. Many White students believe that their hard work is one of the major reasons they landed at a top university; or that their parents' decision to live in an all-White neighborhood had nothing to do with race, racism, or enclaves established by White rage; and that their privilege—if they recognize it—will not have any impact on their students, because they "love kids," "want to make a difference," and/or "have wanted to be a teacher since they were little girls playing school with their dolls." How can you love something you know so little about? When 88 percent of all teachers in schools are White women, conversations that unpack and challenge their ideas about race, class, privilege, meritocracy, religion, sexuality, sexism, and power are critical to the everyday lives of dark children. If the system is just, then who is to blame for poverty, failing schools, crime, and high unemployment? I use the word "blame" intentionally because blame assigns responsibility, and as a former teacher and current teacher educator, I have experienced teachers blaming students—blaming eight-year-olds for falling behind—and not the educational survival complex. If we do not know who or what is responsible, then how do we abolish it—how and where do we fight?

Too often, future educators and those teaching in the field conclude that dark children and their families are solely responsible for their life conditions. There is no interrogation or indictment of the system; it is all about personal responsibility and merit. So, when a five-year-old comes to school not reading at a first-grade level like his rich, White counterparts, he is deemed behind in the minds of educators. A working mom is labeled a "bad" parent who does not "care about her kid(s)" because she works and cannot be reached by phone. Parents who risk it all to come to this country for a better life for their children are somehow seen as "undeserving" of America's minimum-wage jobs, which in some places pay only $5.15 an hour. Without fail, every year in one of my teacher education classes, a student says, "I heard some parents don't care about their kids." When I ask who else has heard such a thing, almost all of my students raise their hands. But when I ask how many have actually witnessed this phenomenon, maybe two raise their hands. And when I ask the two students to say more, their responses are still hearsay. So how do we undo what has been done? How do we not only shift thinking but prepare teachers to have the knowledge, language, and understanding to see past ideas of individualized blame and understand the complexities of systemic oppression? The answer: teachers must embrace theory to help fill the teacher education gap.

THE NORTH STAR

Polaris is often called the North Star; it is one of the brightest stars in the sky. Even when a full moon masks the starry skies, the North Star can still be seen. It never changes position—it always points north. For enslaved folx fleeing bondage, the North Star marked the way to freedom. Abolitionists used the North Star to guide escaping enslaved folx north to places like Rochester, New York. It was a constant reminder to freedom-dream. Theory is my North Star: it is a steadfast tool to explain without fluff or gimmicks what I am experiencing first as a human being and then as a Black lesbian living in the US. Theory helps explain and examine our reality and our students' realities. The context (i.e., their block, neighborhood, community, city) in which students learn in 2019 is not the world they created or chose. Students' community realities were not determined by them or their parents, so teachers have to know more than students' everyday realities. Teachers need to have the backstory of the community and why change is so hard because of patterns of injustice reproduced by established systems and structures of inequality. Theory consistently explains patterns of injustice when sound bites, flamboyant yet hollow teaching practices, and myths about dark people block ideas of humanity, justice, and dignity. Theory is a "location for healing," like the North Star.

Theory does not solve issues—only action and solidarity can do that—but theory gives you language to fight, knowledge to stand on, and a humbling reality of what intersectional social justice is up against. Theory lets us size up our opponent, systemic injustice. Theory is a practical guide to understanding injustice historically, the needs of people, and where collective power lives within groups of people. There are many useful theories that explain the world in a way that helps me break down injustice in small, digestible pieces. Without theory, the moveable mountain of injustice and oppression seems too big and immobile, but theory helps us understand that our job is not to move mountains but to outmaneuver them. For all those reasons, I will use space in this chapter to introduce some theories and highlight how they provide an understanding of injustice concerning particular groups inside and outside an educational context.

WHO WAS HERE FIRST AND WHY IT MATTERS

I hope by now we all know that Columbus did not discover America, and Indigenous people were killed, tortured, and spirit-murdered for their land. These historical facts may seem like just that, historical. But scholars like Eva Tuck, K. Wayne Yang, Patrick Wolfe, and Leigh Patel remind us that settler colonialism "is a structure, not an event," meaning that settler colonialism is a theory that helps to frame how destroying, then taking, Indigenous land is a ceaseless, ongoing project.[8]

For Indigenous people in the US, invasion is a constant. For example, the Indian Removal Act of 1830, signed by President Andrew Jackson, forcibly removed Indigenous people from their land so that White settlers could become slave masters and profit from Indigenous land and free labor. Schools teach this intentional ethnic cleansing as the Trail of Tears, and that is often where the story ends. However, the Homestead Act of 1862 gave 270 million acres of land west of the Mississippi to White settlers. In 1949, the Hoover Commission recommended the "termination" of Native reservations so they could be converted into major cities; by 1952, the "House Joint Resolution 698 established criteria and guidelines for the termination of trustee status of Indian tribes and reservations."[9] In 1972, almost two hundred Indians mobilized and caravanned from the West Coast to Washington, DC. Referring to themselves as the Trail of Broken Treaties Caravan, they demanded to present President Nixon with their twenty-point declaration that ordered the United States to respect the sovereignty of Indian Nations. These premeditated moves—and many more—to push Indians out of their native lands are masked by fake holidays like Thanksgiving Day and Columbus Day, which depict Indian Nations willfully giving their food, cattle, and land to White men. The truth is, the taking of Indigenous land by the US government never stopped. The theory of settler colonialism is defined this way:

> Settler colonialism is a structure, not an event. This means that settler colonialism is not something that happened in history. It is an ongoing and ever-changing structure that defines everything in settler states. . . . In this moment, the project of settler colonialism is defined by resource extraction and development on Indigenous lands in the name of progress. Resource extraction—like coal mining, oil drilling, pipelines, fracking, uranium and copper mining, etc.—have disproportionately negative health, cultural, and economic consequences for Indigenous people and lands. Settler colonialism is always about moving land into the hands of a few and always through violent means.[10]

Applying the settler-colonialism theory to the present day is not hard. In 2015, plans were approved to start construction on Energy Transfer Partners' Dakota Access Pipeline. The pipeline stretches over 1,172 miles long, cost over $3.78 billion to build, and carries hydraulically fractured crude oil from the Bakken oil fields in western North Dakota to southern Illinois, crossing beneath the Missouri and Mississippi Rivers, as well as Lake Oahe, near the Standing Rock Indian Reservation. Initial blueprints planned for the pipeline to cross under the predominantly White town of Bismarck, North Dakota. That plan was rejected because of the pipeline's close proximity to the town's municipal water sources. The pipeline was then rerouted to run beneath Standing Rock's water supply and ancient burial grounds. Why was it acceptable to run fractured crude oil beneath Standing Rock's water supply but not Bismarck's?

The move violated United States environmental regulations and the Treaty of Fort Laramie of 1868 (also called the Sioux Treaty), as well as the Treaty of Fort Laramie of 1851. Standing Rock elders led an international protest against the pipeline. People from all over the world descended on Standing Rock to stand in solidarity with protecting the reservation's clean water, burial grounds, and sovereignty.

Bulldozers, attack dogs, water cannons, armed soldiers, and police in riot gear destroyed the protesters' camp blocking the pipeline's path. Through violent means, land was taken and the pipeline was installed. According to reports, the Dakota Access Pipeline leaked five times in 2017.[11]

Settler colonialism is a lens that helps us understand how Native Americans experience systemic oppression in the United States in a different way than any other dark group. The constant theft of Indigenous land, the extraction of resources, and the cultural genocide of Indigenous people has led to "negative health, cultural, and economic consequences for Indigenous people and lands."[12] In terms of schooling, the US enacted cultural and linguistic genocide of Native American students. Indigenous children were taken from their families and put in boarding schools that viewed them as savages. In order to survive, they had to let go of their language, cultural traditions, and spiritual practices: cultural genocide. Cultural genocide through education is also another tactic for land invasion. Settler-colonialism theory helps us understand oppression beyond race or class and adds the constant invasion of land to the conversation and ideas of intersectional social justice.

VAMPIRES AND RACISM

People say that racism will die out when all the old racist White men are dead. I guess old racist White men are vampires because racism is alive and well. So, what explains how racism is reproduced, generation after generation, in the midst of the country becoming more technologically advanced, with some of the most elite colleges in the world, and a prideful reputation for diversity (when it makes the country look good for a model of democracy)? Critical race theory, often referred to by its acronym, CRT, critiques how power is maintained century after century through capitalism and racism, while laws are passed that promise equality. During the 1980s, legal scholars such as Derrick Bell, Kimberlé Crenshaw, Richard Delgado, and Lani Guinier started to question the so-called "gains" and "progress" of the civil rights movement. They found that despite legal solutions intended to address racism and move the US toward equality, racism and discrimination persisted in all the fundamental institutions that make this country run, such as education, housing, banking, employ- ment, and healthcare.[13]

The field of education embraced CRT in the late 1990s when scholars were looking for ways to "work against racism in educa- tion."[14] CRT is a tool to "expose hidden systemic and customary ways in which racism works by drawing from a wide variety of sources of knowledge that range from statistics to social science research to personal experience."[15] CRT works to understand the centrality of racism—meaning that racism is permanent and understanding it is fundamental to understanding how all structures are organized in the US. For critical race theorists, racism is at the center of understand- ing oppression, which is also linked to gender, class, and citizenship status. CRT challenges color-blindness, meritocracy, and neutrality. CRT also centers knowledge that derives from dark peoples' expe- riences with racism by using counter-stories, which challenge the normalization of the White worldview of knowledge while affirming the personal and family histories of dark people. CRT pushes to the forefront dark people's intimate knowledge of racism as a tool to chal- lenge it and as a space of collective power and resistance.[16] Lastly, CRT argues that racial remedies for equality can happen only if these remedies benefit White people and their interests. Derrick Bell called this proposition "interest convergence." A good example of interest convergence is school desegregation: a disproportionate amount of money that went to desegregating schools in the South during the late 1950s and 1960s was directed toward White schools that enrolled Black children. Thus, White schools profited from receiving Black students, while Black teachers were replaced by White teachers.

Another manifestation of "interest convergence" is the fact that White women have benefited from affirmative action more than any other group. For example, "a 1995 report by the California Senate Government Organization Committee found that White women held a majority of managerial jobs (57,250) compared with African Americans (10,500), Latinos (19,000), and Asian Americans (24,600) after the first two decades of affirmative action in the private sector."[17] More current data show that, in 2015, "a disproportionate representation of White women business owners set off concerns that New York state would not be able to bridge a racial gap among public contractors."[18] Simply put, "interest convergence" argues that White people will support civil rights legislation only when it's in their interest to do so.

CRT is such a useful tool in understanding how racism functions in our schools, communities, and laws that offshoots have sprung up. Latinx CRT (LatCrit) provides an analysis of how racism functions in relation to immigration status, language, and culture. Latinx CRT understands that the US government separating children from their families at the border with Mexico and throwing these children in cages like property is a vile tactic that is not new to America; this *is* America. Native American children were taken, African children were taken, and Japanese children were taken and put into internment camps. CRT scholars conclude that the US will always see non-Whites as property; this country was founded on slaves being seen as property, not human beings. Children being taken, caged, and/or sold is America's history.

Asian CRT (AsianCrit) examines immigration policies and the use of the "model minority" stereotype as a form of anti-Blackness. Feminist CRT (FemCrit) investigates the gendered oppression dark people experience. White CRT (WhiteCrit) examines race, racism, racial identity, and the workings of White privilege.

Although conversations involving intersectionality are burgeoning in the field of education, the connections among race, racism, and dis/ability have not gotten much traction. Dis/ability critical race studies (DisCrit) examines how dark students are overrepresented in special education, overrepresented among those labeled emotionally disturbed, and overrepresented among those labeled learning disabled, and criminalized for being dis/abled. Subini Ancy Annamma's book *The Pedagogy of Pathologization: Dis/abled Girls of Color in the School-Prison Nexus* uses first-person narratives to explore how the intersections of race, disability, and gender make dark girls a target for the school-to-prison-pipeline.[19] DisCrit expands our understanding of how racism functions and the need for a racialized lens when working with students of color who have dis/abilities.

Although critical race theorists articulate the permanence of racism, their main goal is to abolish racism by drawing on and utilizing the resources of dark communities. One way to examine the resources of dark communities is through what critical race theorist Tara Yosso calls "community cultural wealth."[20] Yosso stresses that there are six types of cultural capital that educators should understand and use to empower students beyond White narratives of what cultural capital is and is not.

1. Aspirational—that dark folx continue to have "hopes and dreams" despite persistent, structural barriers in education, employment, housing, and healthcare
2. Linguistic—the beautiful and rich storytelling and communication skills of linguistically diverse students
3. Familial—how family members' wisdom, stories, and traditions can be a positive resource
4. Social capital—using your network for accessing college and other social institutions
5. Navigational—how dark people have to maneuver hostile spaces to be successful despite being unsupported
6. Resistance—recognizes that dark folx are committed in the fight for justice and abolitionist work[21]

Yosso's community cultural wealth theory is primarily focused on dark students gaining access to college but I think the theory extends beyond college to the everyday lives of dark folx living and learning on the margins of society. For example, dark folx' aspirations are what freedoms are made of because they dream despite having every reason in the world not to. Dark parents want the best for their children; we must always remember that. Patty wanted the best for me. She did not have a blueprint of what that looked like in real terms, such as college tuition, recommendation letters, and employment, but she believed in me and this flawed system. Her wisdom was in helping me to un-derstand how to navigate hostile spaces as a little Black girl, which became one of my greatest strengths. Using Yosso's community cul-tural wealth model helps teachers find dark children's strength within their community and within themselves. I found those things earlier in my life through FIST, Mr. Clayton, Mrs. Johnson, Mrs. Knight, Coach Nally, Mrs. James, Karen, my friends, my family, and learning that I could resist.

CRT combined with community cultural wealth not only pro-vides an intellectual space to critique racism and understand how it operates in a world with laws that seem just, but also how to empower communities to recognize and affirm the wealth they already have to fight racism.

FEMINISM IS FOR BLACK WOMEN AND ALL MEN TOO (IT ALWAYS HAS BEEN)

In March 2017, a number of Black and Latinx girls went missing from the nation's capital in a two-week period. Community members were outraged and demanded that local police provide answers. On March 22, a town hall meeting was called with the district's chief of po-lice. The meeting was standing room only, filled to the brim with concerned parents, students, and community members. When all the pictures and live video from the town hall hit the Internet, one thing was clear: there were few, if any, White people there. However, al-most exactly two months before (on January 21, 2017), the Women's March, the largest demonstration for women's and human rights ever in the US, took place in Washington, DC. But the All Lives Matter folx were nowhere to be found at the town hall meeting, and White feminists were missing en masse. Situations like the one I am describ-ing are not new or unusual. Typically, when there is a rally called for dark girls, the country goes mute.

However, Black feminists such as bell hooks, Audre Lorde, So-journer Truth, Patricia Hill Collins, Cynthia B. Dillard, Charlene Car-ruthers, Barbara Smith, Andrea J. Ritchie, Brittney C. Cooper, Treva Lindsey, Alicia Garza, Ruth Nicole Brown, Venus Evans-Winters, Joan Morgan, and Melissa Harris-Perry have all fought, written, and organized around the understanding that "women who theorize the experiences and ideas shared by ordinary Black women provide a unique angle of vision on self, community, and society."[22] Black feminism provides an analysis of misogyny, sexism, and patriarchy—along with the intersections of race, class, sexuality, and gender—to disrupt and challenge racialized gender oppression while creating strategies for resistance and community thriving. Black feminism is a theory that mandates practice. Black feminism is not just theoretical, it is an everyday practice of engaging with individuals and of communities centering the lives of dark girls and women. Black feminists deeply care about their communities. Black feminism is not antimale, it is for all individuals who understand what Malcolm X once said: "The most disrespected woman in America is the Black woman. The most unprotected person in America is the Black woman. The most neglected person in America is the Black woman."[23] Frances E. W. Harper said, "Black women need the [right to] vote, not as a form of education, but as a form of protection." Black feminism centers Black women and girls, and girls of color, because there is an understanding that "racism alone as a phenomenon in the lives of Black women was politically insufficient as an analysis or as a plan of action."[24] Intersectionality grew out of Black feminism because it is "crucial to understand the particular experiences of Black women as compared to White women and Black men, but it also created entry points for Black women to engage in politics."[25]

Black feminism is concerned about the lives of those deemed most disposable by society: dark children, dark queer and trans folx, and women all along the gender spectrum. Black feminism organizes and creates community from a space of Black joy. Black Lives Matter, an organization founded by three Black queer women, demonstrates the power, influence, and real-life outcomes of Black feminism.

IT'S MORE THAN WHO LIKES WHO

In 2010, syndicated columnist and author Dan Savage, along with his partner, Terry Miller, both White men, uploaded a video to You-Tube hoping to inspire LGBTQ youth to stay resilient and hopeful as they experience verbal and physical harassment in their schools, communities, and/or homes. Savage's video was the lynchpin for the international campaign It Gets Better. As the campaign's popularity skyrocketed, celebrities, politicians, and activists posted videos encouraging youth to stay strong and imagine going off to college, leaving bullies behind, or moving away from their small, homophobic town to the diverse, gay-friendly big city. It Gets Better's simplistic and disingenuous metanarrative argued that once high school ends, miraculously all bullying stops and homophobia is somehow subdued in urban America. It Gets Better, with all the bells and whistles of social media and celebrity star power, revamped the old message of: pull yourself up by your bootstraps and live the heteronormative (that is, the idea that the traditions of heterosexuals are the norms for all members of society) dream of children and marriage.[26]

Equally significant to the heteronormative critiques of It Gets Better, the campaign also Whitewashed queerness. "Queer" is a widely used catchall term in the LGBTQ community. It can describe someone's sexuality or nonconforming gender identity, or it can be used to reject labels and binaries (male, female) altogether, but the word also functions as a space to think, act, perform, create, and be outside what is considered "normal," particularly what White, straight, middle-class America says is normal. It Gets Better's aspirational claims that queer life gets better were solely for White, young, gay men who are middle class to wealthy.

There was not much queer about It Gets Better other than sexuality, and queer is much more than who you love, marry, or have sex with. The monolithic norming of the campaign overlooked and ignored the experiences of dark queer youth, poor queer youth, dark poor queer youth, queer youth who are undocumented, dark queer youth with dis/abilities, and Muslim queer youth. The campaign centered Whiteness, exclusively.[27] According to Michael Johnson Jr., queer youth of color in the It Gets Better videos "appear infrequently if at all, and rarely are such messages addressed to the unique plight that queer youth of color face in American society."[28] It Gets Better's treatment of dark queer youth is symptomatic of society at large. For example, a report by the advocacy group Advocates for Youth found that 42 percent of homeless youth are queer; however, 65 percent of queer homeless youth are racial minorities. The report also found that queer youth of color admitted experiencing victimization in schools, either because of race or sexual identity; in the same report, more than a third of queer youth said they experienced physical violence. Queer youth of color, particularly dark queer youth, "grow up in a hegemonic White world, living on the periphery of a White-dominant society, ostracized both for their sexual desires and racial identity."[29]

It Gets Better is a good example of why we need theory that centers sexuality as well as race, gender, class, and other identities. Black queer studies is an important field for understanding sexuality in relationship to other identities. The need for Black queer studies came about because queer studies and queer theory ignored the concerns of queer Black people. Political scientist and Black feminist Cathy Cohen suggests that "queer theorizing that calls for the elimination of fixed categories of sexual identity seems to ignore the ways in which some traditional social identities and communal ties can, in fact, be important to one's survival."[30] Queer theory must address how dark people and queer dark people build community together to survive homophobia, racism, classism, and possibilities for intersectional social justice.

This need is why E. Patrick Johnson coined the term "quare" studies.[31] Johnson defines quare in part as

—*adj.* 2. a lesbian, gay, bisexual, or transgendered person of color who loves other men or women, sexually or nonsexually, and appreciates black culture and community.

—*n.* 3. one who *thinks* and *feels* and *acts* (and, sometimes, "acts up"); committed to struggle against all forms of oppression—racial, sexual, gender, class, religious, etc.

—*n.* 4. one for whom sexual and gender identities always already intersect with racial subjectivity.

—*n.* 5. quare is to queer as "reading" is to "throwing shade."[32]

Resistance and loving Blackness are essential elements of quare studies. You do not have to be lesbian, or a gay person, or a bisexual individual, or identify as transgendered to use and/or be quare. Quare studies is interested in the ways dark people subvert spaces, identities, and resources to ensure our survival. We all need quare studies as a lens for liberation, freedom, and abolitionism.

STUDYING WHITE FOLX AND RACISM

Racism does not exist without Whiteness. Whiteness is at the center of the reproduction of structural inequality. White folx truly concerned about understanding racism, about being in solidarity with dark folx, about building community, and who are interested in intersectional justice have to start with learning about Whiteness and how it functions. Critical White Studies (CWS) is a body of scholarship that aims to underscore how White supremacy and privilege are often invisible in society yet are still reproduced. For example, CWS questions how some European-based groups (such as Italians, the Irish, and Jews) became White in America. CWS also looks beyond skin color to ideas of how race is constructed and asks critical questions, such as, "What is Whiteness without Blackness?" In addition to CWS, "dysconscious racism," a term coined by education researcher Joyce King, describes the habits, perceptions, attitudes, and beliefs that justify racial inequality, the social and economic advantages of being White, and White privilege that does not allow alternative visions of society.[33] Dysconscious racism is practiced by teachers who want to celebrate diversity with holidays, food, and cultural artifacts but never challenge their assumptions about dark people and how Whiteness is reproduced for their advantage.[34] Dysconscious racists are the folx who say "I do not see color," denying their students' racial experiences, cultural heritage, and ways of resistance. Color-blindness is racist.

Another useful tool to understanding why addressing Whiteness is such a difficult task for White people is Robin DiAngelo's concept of "White fragility." This theory states that when White people are confronted with minimum amounts of racial stress, which could be a conversation about race and racism in America, their initial reactions are to become angry, fearful, or guilty.[35] This range of emotions leads to argumentation, silence, or leaving the stressful situation with more stress than at the onset. Adding to DiAngelo's work is the concept of "White emotionality," developed by Cheryl E. Matias. White emotionality goes a step further than White fragility by arguing that when race and racism raise up emotions of guilt, shame, anger, denial, sadness, dissonance, and disconcert, those feelings need to be deeply investigated to understand how racialized emotions perpetuate racism.[36] Many conversations, courses, and professional development sessions focused on addressing and challenging racism and privilege with White people end in frustration because White emotionality is never discussed or dealt with. Before we try to teach White people how to work to undo their privilege, we must start with the emotions of that process—understanding that the emotional process is step one.

White folx cannot be coconspirators until they deal with the emotionality of being White. A cofounder of Black Lives Matter, Alicia Garza, says, "Co-conspiracy is about what we do in action, not just in language." She adds, "It is about moving through guilt and shame and recognizing that we did not create none of this stuff. And so what we are taking responsibility for is the power that we hold to transform our conditions."[37] Studying Whiteness, White rage, and violence is a fundamental step to moving from ally to coconspirator.

WHAT LIES BENEATH

As Americans, we hear talk all the time about the privatization of our healthcare system, prisons, teacher pensions, schools, and Veterans Affairs. The central idea of privatization is to end governmental interventions such as President Franklin Roosevelt's New Deal and social services that provide a safety net for everyone who is not rich, especially the truly poor. The privatization of America's governmental services and the elimination of "the public good" or "community" is what economists call neoliberalism.[38] Corporate school reformers are an indispensable part of the neoliberal machine gutting our dark public schools and their communities.

The teacher strikes of 2018 have everything to do with neoliberalism. The neoliberal agenda in terms of public education is decades old. School districts such as Chicago's have been experiencing deep budget cuts, mass closures of neighborhood schools, and an increase in charter schools, creating competition for the city's poorest neighborhood schools, for years.[39] Instead of adequately funding schools, ensuring teachers have the resources and support to teach dark children beyond survival, and increasing teacher pay, school districts and city governments sustain the educational survival complex. For example, in Chicago in 2012, the city gave a gigantic $528 million tax break to the Chicago Mercantile Exchange; at the same time, teachers went on strike demanding increased wages, more training, protection of teacher benefits, and fair evaluation procedures. The strike was championed by abolitionist Karen Lewis, president of the Chicago Teachers Union, who has been fighting the neoliberal education reform model for years. Lewis stated, "Although we don't control the policies, curriculum or purse strings, educators must be in the forefront of developing education policy, not politicians and venture capitalists."[40] She added, "Parents, teachers, paraprofessionals, and community leaders can no longer afford to wait for the Chicago Board of Education to give us educational justice. We must advocate for the schools our children deserve."[41] This is how an educational abolitionist speaks in the face of neoliberalism.

To be clear, neoliberalism is making inroads all over the world. The main thrust of this idea is that competition is good for the economy, that the free market will solve all of our financial and social problems, and that deregulation is best, regardless of how it impacts the environment or job safety. Neoliberalism has put our banks, roads, schools, hospitals, waterways, and highways at risk. We no longer care about the common good for everyone; we leave everything up to the free market and people's so-called merit/hard work. Neoliberalism ensures that the rich get richer and the poor get disposed of. Neoliberalism is a tool of dark suffering. Patricia Hill Collins wrote, "Contemporary forms of oppression do not routinely force people to submit. Instead, they manufacture consent for domination so that we lose our ability to question and thus collude in our own subordination."[42] Neoliberalism puts already oppressed groups in competition with one another instead of building solidarity bonded by injustice and resistance. Understanding neoliberalism is an important lens to understanding how society keeps us at odds with each other and fighting over the scraps left after the rich have gutted systems that are supposed to help those with the least.

WHAT I HAVE LEARNED

Theory is one of the most important tools I have been able to use to help me understand the possibilities and the limitations of public education and the nonprofit sector. I have had the opportunity to view education from various levels as a student, a teacher, a teacher educator, a parent, and a board member and chair of a charter school, where I sat on hiring committees for teachers and principals, managed grievances, did my best to understand school budgets, navigated an unpredictable school district relationship, and dealt with so-called scandals. Make no mistake, I did not learn as quickly as I would have liked that the ability of education to be a mechanism for freedom, particularly for dark students, is suspended in midair by Whiteness, racism, sexism, and neoliberalism.

When you understand how these theories function, when they become your North Star, you understand why progress is so hard and why survival is a constant struggle. Theories are more than just academic words that folx with degrees throw around at coffee shops and poetry slams; they work to explain to us how the world works, who the world denies, and how structures uphold oppression. It is not by chance or good fortune that top-level staff at nonprofits and charter schools are overwhelmingly White people serving dark populations, who deserve more than a five-year strategic plan and dreams of saving all the less fortunate. Dark families deserve and have a right to the power of the organization that seeks to determine what is the right course of action for their lives. Meaning the decision-making, the budget, the staff, and the overall goals should be made in conjunction with the community and with an analysis of Whiteness, racism, sexism, homophobia, and neoliberalism.

All the decisions we make must be guided by our moral compass of intersectional social justice. Where we choose to live, teach, send our kids to school, work, go to the movies, dine, and attend college, as well as the TV shows we watch, the clothes we buy, and even where we buy goods can all be traced back to race, racism, Whiteness, classism, sexuality, gender, and whose land we are living on. If our everyday repetitive, mundane life decisions are made by racism, Whiteness, and sexism, then so are our curriculums, discipline policies, teacher hiring practices, school-closing decisions, testing, teacher pay, teacher turnover, and school leaders. The struggle for educational freedom does not somehow vanish when you apply theory, but your barriers are no longer hiding in plain sight; now you have the language, understanding, and, hopefully, coconspirators not only to fight but also to demand what is needed to thrive. Understanding theory does not

mean you live an oppressive life. It means you have a deep under-standing of oppression and how it works structurally. However, what you are learning about are people's real lives. You theorize it, while some people live it. I often conduct workshops on racism and White supremacy, topics that make many of my participants uncomfortable. I remind them that it's okay to be uncomfortable but also to under-stand that while you may be uncomfortable for forty-five minutes, other people are uncomfortable their entire lives dealing with oppres-sion. Theory explains what we see; it can take the Whiteness glasses from our eyes.

This powerful and telling drawing by J. David Edwards demon-strates why we need theory. Without theory most of us, not just White people, are wearing what Edwards calls "White Vision Glasses." Teachers spirit-murder children every day through these glasses be-cause their vision is impaired by hate, racism, and White supremacy; they cannot see Black joy or Black humanity. James Baldwin said, "A child cannot be taught by anyone who despises him, and a child can-not afford to be fooled."[43] As long as teachers turn to gimmicks and not the North Star, they will never understand how they are being fooled by White supremacy, patriarchy, homophobia, and classism, and how their so-called accountability measures really show dark children how much education despises them.

CHAPTER 7

WE GON' BE ALRIGHT, BUT THAT AIN'T ALRIGHT

The Negro American consciousness is not a product (as so often seems true of so many American groups) of a will to historical forgetfulness. It is a product of our memory, sustained and constantly reinforced by events, by our watchful waiting, and by our hopeful suspension of final judgments as to the meaning of our grievances.

—RALPH ELLISON[1]

PUNCHING BAG

I started having panic attacks after my kids were born. At first I thought I was experiencing the warning signs of a stroke. Heart disease runs in my family, so I was convinced my bad genes were starting to show the signs, and at the age of thirty I thought my life was coming to an end. The disease that took my father, both of my grandmothers, and put all my siblings on high-blood-pressure medication was finally coming for me. I made appointment after appointment with cardiologists. Everything came back normal, sometimes better than normal. But normal results only caused more stress. I was committed to the idea that I was dying a slow death. I worked out, ate healthy, got my affairs in order, and took out two additional life insurance policies. My partner and I had just bought our first house, we had two beautiful healthy babies (twins), and my career was taking off. By American standards of success, I was right on track. I was living the American queer dream, minus the dog (I am allergic): two kids, a home, white-picket fence, and a beautiful wife. We also had and still have an amazing, supportive friends-and-family network that cares for us, so on the check list of arbitrary life goals, the Loves were winning.

Since life was so good, I could not understand why I was so stressed out. I had nothing to be stressed out about, so it had to be heart disease. It was the only thing that made sense. Until my mother told me she was experiencing panic attacks. Patty? How could the toughest person on the planet suffer from panic attacks? To my knowledge, my mother has never been afraid of anything or anyone. I am sure she has fears but she never expressed them openly to me: as a Black mother she is not supposed to. She has always been a rock of confidence and pride. Patty makes a way out of no way. She is a survivor because Patty may be down, but she is never out. Her strength is incredible. Of course, Patty is not superhuman; she is a Black mother, which the world has decided means a superwoman. Patty was told as a little girl, and it was reinforced when she became a mother, that she could never crack, could never show pain, hurt, or vulnerability; it is her birthright to carry America's racism, sexism, and inequalities on her shoulders and never stress about it. To be a Black mother is to be America's punching bag, as you morph into a shield and take every blow for your family, especially your Black children, that will be thrown by America's White rage. After decades of Patty enduring America's abuse, her shell was cracking, and as a new mom of two beautiful Black children, my tough shell, which I learned from Patty and grew through America's hate, was cracking too. We were running out of grit.

WE FEEL NO PAIN BECAUSE WE FEEL EVERYTHING

Racism is literally killing Black women and their babies. In the spring of 2018, Linda Villarosa of the *New York Times* wrote a heart-wrenching article meticulously detailing how "Black infants in America are now more than twice as likely to die as White infants—a racial disparity that is actually wider than in 1850, 15 years before the end of slavery, when most Black women were considered chattel."[2]

The article goes on to rightfully contend that Black women are dying during pregnancy because of the racism they experience inside and outside of labor rooms. In the 1960s the United States ranked twelfth in Black infant mortality rates among developed countries; fifty-plus years later, the US is now thirty-second out of the thirty-five wealthiest nations.[3] Villarosa goes on to explain that "education and income offer little protection" for Black women.[4] For example, a Black woman with an advanced degree is more likely to lose her baby than a White woman with less than an eighth-grade education. Black women are four times more likely to die from pregnancy-related causes than White women. Tennis star and multi-millionaire Serena Williams described to the world on her Facebook page how her concerns were ignored by the medical staff while she was giving birth to her first child. Williams has a well-documented history of pulmonary embolism, the sudden blockage of an artery in the lung by a blood clot. Blood clots are common side effects when giving birth by caesarean section. After she was treated, but still suffering, surgery revealed that Williams had a large hematoma, a collection of blood, in her abdomen. Williams needed more surgeries and spent six weeks bedridden. The disregard of her concerns and her medical history put her life in danger. Williams's story is that of thousands of Black mothers fighting for their lives and the lives of their children at one of the most vulnerable times in a woman's life. And Williams is a world-renowned athlete who has access to far more resources than most. What explains this type of Black death? Racism. Villarosa writes:

> The reasons for the black-white divide in both infant and maternal mortality have been debated by researchers and doctors for more than two decades. But recently there has been growing acceptance of what has largely been, for the medical establishment, a shocking idea: For black women in America, an inescapable atmosphere of societal and systemic racism can create a kind of toxic physiological stress, resulting in conditions—including hypertension and pre-eclampsia—that lead directly to higher rates of infant and

maternal death. And that societal racism is further expressed in a pervasive, longstanding racial bias in health care—including the dismissal of legitimate concerns and symptoms—that can help explain poor birth outcomes even in the case of black women with the most advantages.[5]

Research shows that White medical students believe that Black people's blood coagulates quicker than Whites, that Black skin is thicker, and that Blacks have less-sensitive nerve endings. Simply put, White doctors believe that Blacks do not feel pain. So, either Black folx are superhuman or not human at all. This is how Black folx are seen and treated as disposable. This is how unarmed Black people get shot or strangled to death by the police or other White men, because White people believe we feel no pain and we have strength beyond the average human.

On the witness stand, Darren Wilson, the cop who shot and killed eighteen-year-old Michael Brown in Ferguson, Missouri, compared Brown to "Hulk Hogan." However, Mike Brown was six-foot-four and so is Darren Wilson. Brown was 292 pounds; Wilson is 210 pounds. Brown was unarmed and Wilson had a Sig Sauer P229 gun at the time he killed Brown. Wilson said he felt like a "five-year-old" because Brown was so big and strong. Wilson's racist views of Brown's strength is no different from White doctors refusing to give Black people pain medication because they believe Black folx have a higher tolerance for pain, or teachers spirit-murdering dark children because they do not see the value of dark children as human beings *with a future that can one day better their lives and the lives of their White children.*

Black mothers fear for all Black life and for their own too. I was mothering in fear. I am mothering under White rage. How do you mother or father or love under White rage? How do you protect when White rage is always raging? Your number one job as a parent is to protect your children from harm but how do you do that when you cannot protect yourself? My children are eight years old. In their eight years of life, Trayvon Martin, Diana Showman, Tamir Rice, Miriam Carey, Malissa Williams, Darnisha Harris, Laquan McDonald, Jeffrey

Holden, Rekia Boyd, Eric Garner, and Sandra Bland have all died for being Black. I am in a constant state of worry, pain, and anxiety for myself, my children, and my wife. We are not only Black women but also lesbians, which puts three targets on my family's backs. Honestly, I became obsessed with dying. My mind stayed focused on the idea that I would die and leave my children unprepared for the world. I thought about death more than I thought about living. Still, somehow, unsure as to why I was having panic attacks, after all I had seen, cried, and obsessed over in the previous seven years, I entered therapy.

THE POLITICS OF RESPECTABILITY

Therapy was healing for me. I had a Black woman therapist, Dr. Vanhoose, whom I could talk to about racism, dark death, and survivor's guilt without feeling like I had to explain to her what those very real things were. She not only listened to me but she understood. She had a set of experiences that were similar to mine as a Black woman in this world. (As a side note, we do not just need more dark teachers but more mental health professionals too.) I knew my experiences being dark in this country were validated by centuries of data, but it felt good and affirming to say it out loud to a professional and be heard, not as whining or complaining but as someone unraveling because of the omnipresence of racism, sexism, homophobia, and injustice. When I was about thirty thousand words into this book and about a year into therapy, Dr. Vanhoose made a pronouncement that helped me heal and at the same time stunned me: she said I was stuck in survival mode. I had given numerous talks on educational survival and was writing a book on survival but I had never applied the idea to myself. She told me that my obsession with dying stemmed from my refusal to embrace my life as it is now. I was still living like that little girl in Rochester, New York, who could not make any mistakes, who witnessed her community overtaken by drugs and crime, and who had never let her guard down. I did not know how to thrive even as I was writing about it.

The MIT economist Peter Temin concludes that to escape poverty you need almost *twenty years* with nothing going wrong in your life.[6] I was at the twenty-year mark. My father had died when I was seventeen, one of the biggest losses in my life. Since his death, I had not made a single mistake. I had not let anything go wrong in my life. Every decision was calculated. I controlled for every variable, seen and unseen. I trusted no one and stayed on my toes. I somehow instinctually knew that I could not make one mistake—that nothing could go wrong or I would never have the life I dreamed about, which was not much. My dreams were not filled with fancy cars, mansions, and lots of money; I dreamed of a life of comfort. All I wanted was not to live paycheck to paycheck.

I told myself when I left Rochester for college at age seventeen that I would never make the mistakes my parents had made and I would never let this world beat me down. I would win at all costs, always with my integrity intact. Meaning I would outsmart, outmaneuver, and outpace anyone. My worldview was drenched in a politics of respectability; I could avoid racial and gender discrimination and harassment by behaving to White folx' standards for Black folx. Politics of respectability is Black folx' version of being the "model minority"; both were born out of anti-Blackness. As I got older and understood that no level of respectability could save my life or my family's lives, and that I could not control Whiteness, I began to panic. I realized I could not outsmart dark death. My nice respectable routine that I practiced in my head in anticipation of being pulled over by the cops—which started with me "accidentally" pulling out my University of Georgia ID before my driver's license so the cops would see I am an educated dark person, and speaking in my professor's voice, which I do not really have—would not stop me from being killed by a cop. I live in the state where a police officer was caught on a dashboard camera telling a White woman, "We only kill Black people."[7]

I was writing about how being Black was exhausting and living that exhaustion at the same time. I did not know how to thrive. I had everything I had ever wanted and was terrified it all would be taken away from me just for being Black. I could not enjoy the present because I was always worried about the future. Life was a constant chess game that I could no longer manipulate, and now there were additional pieces, my family. When I was the only player on the board I had to worry about, it was stressful but manageable. Now, my chessboard was complicated by the most vulnerable pieces—dark children. And I never really controlled the board at all. America allows only a few dark folx to thrive, and I felt like my time was running out and now my children would be there for my downfall.

Dr. Vanhoose told me that I had not enjoyed my life in years. I had not truly lived in years. I had so much to celebrate but could not do so because I thought everything had an expiration date on it due to racism, sexism, and homophobia. I had never thought of myself as living in survival mode—maybe as an educator but not as my full self. Her words rang in my head. How could I be wrong for being perfect? How could being methodical not be good? Dr. Vanhoose simply telling me to live was freeing. She told me that I needed to work on controlling my thoughts and recommended meditation and mindfulness training. I needed these things in order to be well. I still worry; I still panic but not as much. Her asking me to be well changed how I looked at the world. I could not let the thought of racism take my happiness, as it could take my life too. I had to choose the one I could control. I spent so much time thinking about how to win against racism—a game you cannot win—that I did not spend any time thriving.

ALRIGHT AND WELL (THERE'S A DIFFERENCE)

Toni Cade Bambara's novel *The Salt Eaters* opens with a question that haunts the text's Black female protagonist, Velma Henry, and her community: "Are you sure, sweetheart, that you want to be well?"[8] Velma attempted suicide, overwhelmed by her countless and never-ending responsibilities as a mother, a wife, a civil rights activist, and a leader in the community. Minnie Ransom is the town's healer. Minnie is versed in African and Afro-Caribbean spiritual and healing traditions. Throughout the book, at critical points, Minnie tells Velma and other town members, "A lot of weight when you're well. Now, you just hold that thought."[9] The racial, sexual, and environmental injustices Velma has faced in being everything for everybody have made her sick and left her wanting to end her life. To complicate matters, the people of Velma's community are searching for their wellness but feel beholden to a nuclear plant, where Velma works as a computer programmer, which provides jobs for the community yet is slowly poisoning everyone. Although Velma is the main character who is ill, everyone is sick. In the novel, Bambara positions wellness as a choice, a type of freedom that comes when you let go of your fears and move your anger into a space of healing.

Wellness is wisdom and being well is hard work. Minnie tells Velma, "Give it up, the pain, the hurt, the anger, and make room for the lovely things to rush in and fill you full. Nature abhors a so-called vacuum, don't you know?"[10] Velma has flashbacks to police brutality, her miscarriage, her past lover who was beaten at an antiwar rally and left a quadriplegic, her experiences dealing with gender oppression doing civil rights work, her dissipating marriage, and nuclear destruction. She has to confront her past and her fears of the future to seek wellness. Velma also confronts the pain of her ancestors, who are called the Mud Mothers in the book. She rejects them at first, but once she submits to the Mothers the wounds on her wrist from her attempt at suicide are healed. The Mothers and Minnie provided a space for Velma to heal in her world, which was chaotic and filled with injustice. The ways in which Velma was *holding* her stress, her memories of her life, her emotions of her life, and the memories that were passed down to her, were killing her. She did not know what it meant to be well, and what she was holding on to did not allow her to be well; she was content being alright. Alright will kill you.

The Salt Eaters is a book about healing but healing that centers race, racism, culture, history, gender, community, justice, environmental concerns, and humanity. As abolitionists we must be well; we cannot settle for just being alright. Wellness is a part of social justice work. There must be an inner life that refuses to be treated less than human. I had to choose to be well; I had to choose to have an inner life; I had to choose to be vulnerable, to find my own sovereignty rooted in Black joy, Black love, and humanity regardless of America's hate for me and mine. *The Sovereignty of Quiet: Beyond Resistance in Black Culture* by Kevin Quashie reminds me, "As an identity, Blackness is always supposed to tell us something about race or racism, or about America, or violence and struggle and triumph or poverty and hopefulness. The determination to see Blackness only through a social public lens, as if there were no inner life, is racist—it comes from the language of racial superiority and is a practice intended to dehumanize Black people."[11] Dark folx have to choose to see ourselves beyond our protest, beyond our fight for justice; we are more than just resistance. Fighting for justice shows how human and how loving we are. But to be fully human is to know yourself beyond the fight, to have an inner self that can be quiet and enjoy life.

INTERGENERATIONAL HEALING

In the groundbreaking film *Daughters of the Dust* (1991), written and directed by Julie Dash, the character Nana Peazant speaks these weighty words to her grandson: "I am trying to teach you how to touch your own spirit, Eli."[12] Nana, the matriarch of the family, is helping Eli, her grandson, reconcile his two souls: African and African American, a concept Du Bois called "double consciousness."[13] Nana explains to Eli, whose ancestors were enslaved from West Africa, that their cultural wisdom, memories, and creativity thrive inside him, regardless of his seemingly hopeless reality. Nana is asking Eli to understand that to be well he has to work to recognize the pain of his ancestors and the beauty and resiliency of that pain that lives inside of him. Eli is not alone even if he feels like it because he can "touch your own spirit." Which means that knowing who you are, regardless of what America and this anti-Black world throws at you, is healing. Eli is in search of an emotional, physical, social, and spiritual outlet for his pain, similar to Velma in *The Salt Eaters*. Both Eli and Velma experience the everyday trauma of being dark but also the historical trauma that has been passed down from their ancestors; they cannot heal without addressing their ancestors' trauma and sacrifices, and then their own. Thus, healing must be intergenerational, and healing is different for different people. Dark folx heal in ways that are unrecognizable to White folx because Whiteness is why we are in trauma in the first place. Our healing practices differ from those of

White folx, but we all have to get well. Additionally, while trauma is passed down, so must wisdom be passed down from one generation to the next. We all, especially young people, must learn from our elders. Elders provide firsthand knowledge that cannot always be summed up in a textbook or magazine; abolitionists sit at their elders' feet for guidance and understanding, and to learn from their mistakes. At times abolitionists do more listening than talking, especially in the presence of wise counsel. An abolitionist movement must be intergenerational, filled with generational knowledge from the young and the old. Bakari Kitwana makes it plain, when he writes,

> As long as the older generation fails to understand the new Black youth culture in all of its complexities, and as long as the younger generation fails to see its inherent contradictions, we cannot as community address the urgent crises now upon us, particularly those facing Black American youth. New ways of relieving current forms of oppression can be implemented only when the younger and older generations do so together. Our collective destiny demands it.[14]

Kitwana's words are directed toward the lives of Black Americans, but his message can be placed on the lives of all dark folx trying to undo centuries of pain and trauma while remaining hopeful and freedom dreaming.

For me, I had to center myself and practice being well daily. In no way does being well somehow stop injustice, but it does allow you to be your best self while fighting injustice. Being well helps you fight racism with love, grace, and compassion and frees mental space to freedom-dream and to give them hell, and then retreat to your community of love for support, fulfillment, and nourishment—your homeplace. The goal is to be whole, to bring your full self to the work of abolitionist teaching. It does not mean the work of wholeness is complete, because we are all works in progress; being well is to join others in the fight for humanity and antiracism in love and solidarity. Being well is comforting our internalized White supremacy, sexism, homophobia, transphobia, Islamophobia, classism, ableism, and the rage that comes as a result of these hateful ideas. All of me, every drop of my Blackness—ancestors included—queerness, Black womanness, motherness, and everything else in between, must come to the work of abolitionist teaching because "the day all the different parts of me can come along, we would have what I would call a revolution."[15]

WHITE WELLNESS

Whiteness cannot enter spaces focused on abolitionist teaching. Whiteness is addicted to centering itself, addicted to attention, and making everyone feel guilty for working toward its elimination. Whiteness will never allow true solidarity to take place. Those who cling to their Whiteness cannot participate in abolitionist teaching because they are a distraction, are unproductive, and will undermine freedom at every step, sometimes in the name of social justice. Being an abolitionist means you are ready to lose something, you are ready to let go of your privilege, you are ready to be in solidarity with dark people by recognizing your Whiteness in dark spaces, recognizing how it can take up space if unchecked, using your Whiteness in White spaces to advocate for and with dark people. And you understand that your White privilege allows you to take risks that dark people cannot take in the fight for educational justice. Wendy Kohli says it best: "The times require us to have the courage to be dangerous, at the same time recognizing that there are differential dangers. Not all teachers are at equal risk; much depends on how you are positioned, on your identity(ies), on your particular situation."[16] Abolitionist teaching means putting something on the line in the name of justice. Wanting dark folx to thrive and giving up power and positions in order for dark folx to do so.

The work of recognizing and checking White emotionality is done before you enter dark spaces. White folx have to get well on their own terms before they engage with abolitionist teaching. More than just attending antiracist workshops and culturally relevant pedagogy professional developments, they need to come to terms with what Whiteness is, how violence is needed to maintain it, and how their successes in life are by-products of Whiteness. White folx cannot lose their Whiteness; it is not possible. But they can daily try to deal with and reject the Whiteness that is obsessed with oppressing others, centering itself, and maintaining White supremacy through White rage. Being well and White is rejecting Whiteness for the good of humanity. The same goes for patriarchy, homophobia, sexism, transphobia, Islamophobia, classism, ableism, and xenophobia.

WELLNESS IN SCHOOLS

I have had multiple points of view of education, so I know firsthand that education as we know it cannot save dark children either. At both public and charter schools, I have watched Black joy be squeezed out of students and staff by Whiteness. I have seen how a school founded on the African principles of community and love can be intentionally thrown to the side for standardized testing accountability measures, stringent procedures that confine creativity for students and staff, and the rush to be the White survivor. White folx' approach to antiracism work in schools is checking it off their to-do list. I know White administrators and principals who feel uncomfortable speaking about issues of race and racism, but somehow feel comfortable being in charge of a majority-dark teaching staff and student population. I take issue with White school staff members who shy away from speaking out against racism but have no problem controlling dark minds and bodies.

I know from experience, from years of fighting, that school officials often feel the need to control Black bodies (students, staff, and parents) and schools can never be well under those circumstances. This control seems to stem from dark children always being seen as America's property. For schools to be well, and, therefore, the children in them, schools must place more importance on students' mental, physical, and spiritual health than on any test. If students are not well, test scores do not matter. It breaks my heart to talk to a principal who thinks that because test scores are low the school cannot focus on students' emotional well-being. School officials will put everything before students' actual mental health, not understanding that test scores cannot and will not increase until students are healing from trauma and/or mattering to themselves and their community. I have spoken to leaders of schools who understand how racism, Whiteness, and sexism function in schools and want to do something about it, but addressing these issues would mean letting go of their control of Black bodies, losing power, and admitting that they are part of the problem infecting the school.

For schools to be well, educators need to be well. Educators need free therapy, love, compassion, and healing, and to embrace theories that explain why getting well is so hard. Teacher wellness is critical to creating schools that protect students' potential and function as their homeplace. Educators, students, and parents need to be on a path to wellness together for schools to be sites of healing. Schools cannot be doing just alright; they have to be well by putting everyone's mental health as the first priority and understanding how systems of oppression spirit-murder children.

SURVIVAL VS. FREEDOM

I hate binaries, but I am tired of the long spectrum between survival and freedom. Dark folx' lives are consumed by the two options. We live somewhere between never reaching freedom and never becoming fully comfortable with this reality. When pursuing educational freedom—really, all freedoms—survival cannot be the goal, and finding a place somewhere on the spectrum cannot be, either. The goal must be pursuing freedom at all costs as a collective group of abolitionism-minded people who welcome struggle.

I will end where I started: with W. E. B. Du Bois. Early in Du Bois's career, he proclaimed that America's racism was due to a lack of knowledge. He wrote, "The world was thinking wrong about race, because it did not know. The ultimate evil was stupidity. The cure for it was knowledge based on scientific investigation."[17] He wrote these words in 1894. Ibram X. Kendi reminds us that since then, dark folx have provided countless scientific investigations of our humanity.[18]

We have done everything under the sun to matter to the country. We have fought and died for the country. Sued this country and won our rights. Marched and protested while being hit and remained nonviolent. Sung songs about the strangeness of fruit hanging from trees inspired by our resiliency (grit). We have given speeches that the world heard from a podium in Washington, DC, or Selma, Alabama. We have studied at the best schools in the world and produced a body of work that makes the world better. We create artwork that is a road map to the future of humanity for all. This country kills our babies and we mourn with grace and compassion and use each death as a teaching moment for this country to find its North Star. We teach America every day how to live the words on which they formed this country. As Nikki Giovanni says, "We didn't write a constitution . . . we live one. . . . We didn't say 'We the People' . . . we are one."[19] And we do all of this to just survive. Forty-one years after Du Bois dedicated his life to producing the scientific investigation to prove dark folx deserved to be treated as human, he concluded, "Today there can be no doubt that Americans know the facts; and yet they remain for the most part indifferent and unmoved."[20]

There is only one choice: become an abolitionist parent, teacher, doctor, sanitation worker, lawyer, CEO, accountant, community activist, small business owner, scientist, engineer, and *human*.

ACKNOWLEDGMENTS

"Thank You Master" by Donny Hathaway

"Orange Moon" by Erykah Badu

"You Were Meant for Me" by Donny Hathaway, "All I Do" by Stevie Wonder, "You Bring Me Joy" by Anita Baker, and "You Make Life So Good" by Rahsaan Patterson—CHELS

"Be a Lion" by the cast of The Wiz and "Believe in Yourself" by Lena Horne—CHANCE

"Isn't She Lovely" by Stevie Wonder and "Believe in Yourself" by Lena Horne—LAURYN

"Motherfather" by Musiq—PATTY AND HONEY LOVE

"Count on Me" by Bruno Mars and "Thank You" by Boyz II Men—GUMBEE

"So Fresh, So Clean" by OutKast and "Back in the Day" by Ahmad—GENE

"Home" by MJ Rodriguez, Billy Porter, and Our Lady J—ROCHESTER, NEW YORK

"Best Friend" by Brandy and "F.U.B.U." by Solange—NATINA, DRINA, AND CUTTS

"Friends" by The Carters—VIC, EBONI K., EB SHANTE, ZOOK, ERICKA, GHODLY, YOLO, TREVA, BRANDELYN, CORRIE, HYLA, JOEY, JP, ERICA, JONATHAN, ELITA, TIFFANY (SNAPS), KELLY, ASHLEY, DIALLO, REGINA, JOAN, SHANNON, SARAH, LARA, BILLYE, SHERELL, TORRI, and ANDREA

"Gratitude" by Earth, Wind & Fire—ESPOSITO

"Be Real Black for Me" by Donny Hathaway and Roberta Flack— DR. DILLARD

"Turiya and Ramakrishna" by Alice Coltrane—BELL HOOKS

"Move On Up" by Curtis Mayfield—HUTCHINS CENTER FOR AFRICAN AND AFRICAN AMERICAN RESEARCH AT HARVARD UNIVERSITY

"It's Bigger Than Hip Hop" by Dead Prez—HIPHOP ARCHIVE AND RESEARCH INSTITUTE AT HARVARD UNIVERSITY, DR. MORGAN, AND HAROLD SHAWN

"Black Girl Magic" by Jamila Woods—DR. PEAT

"Americans" by Janelle Monáe—RACHAEL MARKS

"So Much Things to Say" (live performance) by Lauryn Hill— LAURYN HILL

"To Be Young, Gifted, and Black" by Nina Simone—ALL MY FORMER STUDENTS

NOTES

CHAPTER 1: "WE WHO ARE DARK"

1. W. E. B. Du Bois, "Criteria of Negro Art," *Crisis* 32, no. 6 (1926): 290–97. Emphasis added.

2. Keeanga-Yamahtta Taylor, ed., *How We Get Free: Black Feminism and the Combahee River Collective* (Chicago: Haymarket Books, 2017), 4.

3. Jennifer Okwerekwu, "White Male Doctors Earn 35 Percent More Than Black Male Doctors," *STAT*, June 16, 2016, https://www.statnews.com /2016/06/07/physician-pay-gap.

4. Ibid.

5. Lauren Camera, "Black Girls Are Twice as Likely to Be Suspended, in Every State," *US News & World Report*, May 9, 2017, https://www.usnews .com/news/education-news/articles/2017–05–09/Black-girls-are-twice-as -likely-to-be-suspended-in-every-state.

6. Ibid.

7. Ibid.

8. Monique Morris, *Pushout: The Criminalization of Black Girls in Schools* (New York: New Press, 2016).

9. Sarah Hinger, "Police Assault on Black Students in Kentucky Sparks Calls for Reform," *ACLU blog*, November 21, 2017, https://www.aclu.org /blog/racial-justice/race-and-criminal-justice/police-assault-Black-students -kentucky-sparks-calls.

10. Bill Ayers, *Demand the Impossible! A Radical Manifesto* (Chicago: Haymarket Books, 2016).

11. Angela Y. Davis, *Freedom Is a Constant Struggle: Ferguson, Palestine, and the Foundations of a Movement* (Chicago: Haymarket Books, 2016).

12. Ta-Nehisi Coates, *Between the World and Me* (New York: Spiegel and Grau, 2015).

13. Ibid.

14. Michael Roy Hames-García, *Fugitive Thought: Prison Movements, Race, and the Meaning of Justice* (Minneapolis: University of Minnesota Press, 2004).

15. Toni Morrison, "Black Studies Center Public Dialogue," Oregon Public Speakers Collection, Portland State University, May 30, 1975.

16. Valerie Strauss, "Report: Big Education Firms Spend Millions Lobbying for Protesting Policies," *Washington Post*, March 30, 2015, https://www.washingtonpost.com/news/answer-sheet/wp/2015/03/30/report-big-education-firms-spend-millions-lobbying-for-pro-testing-policies/?utm_term=.7904eb3ca919.

17. Aviva Shen, "Private Prisons Spend $45 Million on Lobbying, Rake in $5.1 Billion for Immigrant Detention Alone," *Think Progress*, August 3, 2012, https://thinkprogress.org/private-prisons-spend-45-million-on-lobbying-rake-in-5-1-billion-for-immigrant-detention-alone-b9ef073758be.

18. Data Team, "The Mystery of High Unemployment Rates for Black Americans," *Economist*, August 3, 2017, https://www.economist.com/blogs/graphicdetail/2017/08/daily-chart-1.

19. Michael J. Dumas, "Against the Dark: AntiBlackness in Education Policy and Discourse," *Theory into Practice* 55, no. 1 (2016): 11–19.

20. Ibid., 13.

CHAPTER 2: EDUCATIONAL SURVIVAL

1. James Baldwin, *The Price of the Ticket: Collected Nonfiction, 1948–1985* (New York: St. Martin's Press, 1985).

2. Dennis Kucinich, "Our Political Economy Is Designed to Create Poverty and Inequality," *Nation*, March 6, 2017, https://www.thenation.com/article/our-political-economy-is-designed-to-create-poverty-and-inequality.

3. Rupert Neate, "Richest 1% Own Half the World's Wealth, Study Finds," *Guardian*, November 14, 2017, https://www.theguardian.com/inequality/2017/nov/14/worlds-richest-wealth-credit-suisse.

4. Jessica Dickler, "US Households Now Have Over $16,000 in Credit-Card Debt," CNBC, December 13, 2016, https://www.cnbc.com/2016/12/13/us-households-now-have-over-16k-in-credit-card-debt.html.

5. Rakesh Kochhar and Richard Fry, "Wealth Inequality Has Widened Along Racial, Ethnic Lines Since End of Great Recession," Pew Research Center, December 12, 2014, http://www.pewresearch.org/fact-tank/2014/12/12/racial-wealth-gaps-great-recession.

6. Danielle Douglass-Gabriel, "College Is Not the Great Equalizer for Black and Hispanic Graduates," *Washington Post*, August 17, 2015, https://www.washingtonpost.com/news/wonk/wp/2015/08/17/college-is-not-the-great-equalizer-for-Black-and-hispanic-graduates/?utm_term=.2d91db2a6c74.

7. Jasmine Tucker and Caitlin Lowell, "National Snapshot: Poverty Among Women and Families, 2015," National Women's Law Center Fact Sheet, September 2016, https://nwlc.org/resources/national-snapshot-poverty-among-women-families-2015.

8. Ibid.

9. Jean Anyon, *Ghetto Schooling: A Political Economy of Urban Educational Reform* (New York: Teachers College Press, 1997), 181.

10. James Baldwin, "A Letter to My Nephew," *Progressive*, January 1, 1962, http://progressive.org/magazine/letter-nephew.

11. Marc Lamont Hill, *Nobody: Casualties of America's War on the Vulnerable, from Ferguson to Flint and Beyond* (New York: Simon & Schuster, 2017), 65.

12. Langston Hughes, *The Collected Poems of Langston Hughes* (New York: Vintage Classics, 1994).

13. "Ulysses S. Grant's Reflections on the War," from *Personal Memoirs of U. S. Grant* (1865), Smithsonian Source: Resources for Teaching American History, Primary Sources, http://www.smithsoniansource.org/display/primarysource/viewdetails.aspx?PrimarySourceId=1047, accessed August 14, 2018.

14. Carol Anderson, *White Rage: The Unspoken Truth of Our Racial Divide* (New York: Bloomsbury Publishing, 2016), 2.

15. Jason Byrne, "Ocoee on Fire: The 1920 Election Day Massacre," *Florida History*, November 23, 2014, https://medium.com/florida-history/ocoee-on-fire-the-1920-election-day-massacre-38adbda9666e#.8hdglkpvl.

16. James W. Loewen, *Sundown Towns: A Hidden Dimension of American Racism* (New York: New Press, 2005), 4.

17. Byrne, "Ocoee on Fire."

18. John Nichols, "How ALEC Took Florida's 'License to Kill' Law National," *Nation*, March 22, 2012, https://www.thenation.com/article/how-alec-took-floridas-license-kill-law-national.

19. Timothy B. Tyson, *The Blood of Emmett Till* (New York: Simon & Schuster, 2017).

20. Ibid.

21. Equal Justice Initiative, *Lynching in America: Confronting the Legacy of Racial Terror*, 3rd ed. (Montgomery, AL: EJI, 2017), https://eji.org/reports/lynching-in-america.

22. National Archives, "Search the Compensation and Reparations for the Evacuation, Relocation, and Internment Index," https://www.archives.gov/research/japanese-americans/redress, accessed August 21, 2018.

23. Dara Lind, "The Trump Administration's Separation of Families at the Border, Explained," *Vox*, June 15, 2018, https://www.vox.com/2018/6/11/17443198/children-immigrant-families-separated-parents.

24. Lisa Trei, "Black Children Might Have Been Better Off Without *Brown v. Board*, Bell Says," *Stanford Report*, April 21, 2004, http://news.stanford.edu/news/2004/april21/brownbell-421.html.

25. Adam Fairclough, "The Costs of *Brown*: Black Teachers and School Integration," *Journal of American History* 91, no. 1 (2004): 43–55.

26. Melinda Anderson, "Sixty Years After *Brown v. Board* Black Teachers Are Disappearing—Again," *Ebony*, May 19, 2014, http://www.ebony.com/news-views/sixty-years-after-brown-v-board-Black-teachers-are-disappearing-again-304.

27. Liana Loewus, "The Nation's Teaching Force Is Still Mostly White and Female," *Education Week*, August 15, 2017, https://www.edweek.org/ew /articles/2017/08/15/the-nations-teaching-force-is-still-mostly.html.

28. Ibid.

29. Valerie Strauss, "School Segregation Sharply Increasing, Studies Show," *Washington Post*, September 22, 2012, https://www.washingtonpost .com/blogs/answer-sheet/post/school-segregation-sharply-increasing-studies -show/2012/09/22/5b34111a-04c6-11e2-91e7-2962c74e7738_blog.html?utm _term=.19b3b3183908.

30. Greg Toppo, "GAO Study: Segregation Worsening in U.S. Schools," *USA Today*, May 17, 2016, https://www.usatoday.com/story/news/2016/05/17 /gao-study-segregation-worsening-us-schools/84508438.

31. Ibid.

32. Natalie Holmes and Alan Berube, "City and Metropolitan Inequality on the Rise, Driven by Declining Incomes," *Brookings*, January 14, 2016, https://www.brookings.edu/research/city-and-metropolitan-inequality-on -the-rise-driven-by-declining-incomes.

33. Jim Horn, *Work Hard, Be Hard: Journeys Through "No Excuses" Teaching* (Lanham, MD: Rowman & Littlefield, 2016).

34. Ibid.

35. Civil Rights Project, "Study Finds Many Charter Schools Feeding 'School-to-Prison Pipeline,'" press release, March 16, 2016, https://www .civilrightsproject.ucla.edu/news/press-releases/featured-research-2016/study -finds-many-charter-schools-feeding-school-to-prison-pipeline.

36. Shelby Webb, "Some KIPP Houston Schools Charged Unallowable Fees, Agency Finds," *Houston Chronicle*, June 29, 2017, https://www.houston chronicle.com/news/education/article/KIPP-schools-collected-millions-in -unallowable-11257006.php.

37. Equality of Opportunity Project, "Life Expectancy vs. Income in the United States," http://www.equality-of-opportunity.org/health, accessed July 23 2018.

38. Preston C. Green III et al., "Are We Heading Toward a Charter School Bubble? Lessons from the Subprime Mortgage Crisis," *University of Richmond Law Review* 50 (2015): 783.

39. Alan Singer, "Why Hedge Funds Love Charter Schools," *Washington Post*, June 4, 2014, https://www.washingtonpost.com/news/answer -sheet/wp/2014/06/04/why-hedge-funds-love-charter-schools/?utm_term =.52b16c98b987.

40. Ibid.

41. Ibid.

42. Gloria Ladson-Billings, "From the Achievement Gap to the Education Debt: Understanding Achievement in US Schools," *Educational Researcher* 35, no. 7 (2006): 3–12.

43. Ibid.

44. Clare Kim, "Florida School Threatens to Expel Student over 'Natural Hair,'" MSNBC, November 26, 2016, http://www.msnbc.com/the-last-word-94.

45. Breanna Edwards, "Fla. Charter School Principal Under Fire for 'Racist' Facebook Post," *Root*, August 28, 2017, http://www.theroot.com/fla-charter-school-principal-under-fire-for-racist-fac-1798492705?utm_medium=sharefromsite&utm_source=The_Root_facebook.

46. Ibid.

47. Edwin Rios, "Bullying in Schools Is Out of Control Since Election Day," *Mother Jones*, November 16, 2016, https://www.motherjones.com/politics/2016/11/schools-racism-trump-effect-harassment-bullying.

48. Ibid.

49. Ibid.

50. Ibid.

51. Ibid.

52. Kerry Burke, Esha Ray, and Ben Chapman, "Bronx Teacher Sparks Outrage for Using Black Students in Cruel Slavery Lesson," *Daily News* (NY), February 1, 2018, http://www.nydailynews.com/new-york/education/bronx-teacher-sparks-outrage-cruel-slavery-lesson-article-1.3793930.

53. Christopher Petrella and Justin Gomer, "White Supremacy Is Not an Illness," *Black Perspectives*, December 15, 2016, https://www.aaihs.org/White-supremacy-is-not-an-illness.

54. Ibid.

55. Patricia Williams, "Spirit-Murdering the Messenger: The Discourse of Fingerpointing as the Law's Response to Racism," *University of Miami Law Review* 42 (1987): 127.

56. Bettina L. Love, "'I See Trayvon Martin': What Teachers Can Learn from the Tragic Death of a Young Black Male," *Urban Review* 46, no. 2 (2014): 292–306.

57. Patricia Hill Collins and Sirma Bilge, *Intersectionality* (Hoboken, NJ: John Wiley & Sons, 2016).

58. Ibid., 3.

59. Ibram X. Kendi, *Stamped from the Beginning: The Definitive History of Racist Ideas in America* (London: Hachette UK, 2016).

60. Coates, *Between the World and Me*.

61. Anyon, *Ghetto Schooling*, 3.

CHAPTER 3: MATTERING

1. Toni Morrison, *Song of Solomon* (New York: Random House, 2004).

2. Gary Younge, "Eduardo Galeano: 'My Great Fear Is That We Are All Suffering from Amnesia,'" *Guardian*, July 23, 2013, https://www.theguardian.com/books/2013/jul/23/eduardo-galeano-children-days-interview.

3. Daniel Patrick Moynihan, "The Negro Family: The Case for National Action (1965)," *African American Male Research* (1997). Also, Lee

Rainwater, William L. Yancey, and Daniel Patrick Moynihan, *The Moynihan Report and the Politics of Controversy: A Transaction Social Science and Public Policy Report* (Cambridge, MA: MIT Press, 1967).

4. Marvin Wolfgang and Franco Ferracuti, *The Subculture of Violence: Towards an Integrated Theory in Criminology* (London: Tavistock, 1967).

5. Daniel Geary, "The Moynihan Report Is Turning 50. Its Ideas on Black Poverty Were Wrong Then and Are Wrong Now," *In These Times*, June 20, 2015, http://inthesetimes.com/article/18132/moynihan-report -Black-poverty.

6. bell hooks, *Teaching to Transgress* (New York: Routledge, 1994).

7. Ibid., 2.

8. Ibid., 65.

9. Brittney C. Cooper, *Beyond Respectability: The Intellectual Thought of Race Women* (Urbana: University of Illinois Press, 2017).

10. Jill Rosen, "With Just One Black Teacher, Black Students More Likely to Graduate," Johns Hopkins University news release, April 5, 2017, http://releases.jhu.edu/2017/04/05/with-just-one-Black-teacher-Black-students -more-likely-to-graduate.

11. Barbara Ransby, *Ella Baker and the Black Freedom Movement: A Radical Democratic Vision* (Chapel Hill: University of North Carolina Press, 2003).

12. Edward Telles and Liza Steele, "The Effects of Skin Color in the Americas," *Americas Quarterly* (February 21, 2012), http://americasquarterly .org/the-effects-of-skin-color-in-the-americas.

13. Jonathan White, "Fifty Years Since the Rochester, New York Riots," World Socialist Web Site, September 5, 2014, https://www.wsws.org/en /articles/2014/09/05/roch-s05.html.

14. Peter Applebome, "Despite Long Slide by Kodak, Company Town Avoids Decay," *New York Times*, January 16, 2012, https://www.nytimes .com/2012/01/17/nyregion/despite-long-slide-by-kodak-rochester-avoids -decay.html.

15. Sentencing Project, "Criminal Justice Facts," https://www.sentencing project.org/criminal-justice-facts, accessed August 22, 2018.

16. National Association for the Advancement of Colored People, "Criminal Justice Fact Sheet," http://www.naacp.org/criminal-justice-fact -sheet, accessed August 19, 2018.

17. American Civil Liberties Union, "Facts About the Over-Incarceration of Women in the United States," https://www.aclu.org/other/facts-about -over-incarceration-women-united-states, accessed July 25, 2018.

18. Prison Policy Initiative, *Women's Mass Incarceration: The Whole Pie 2017*, https://www.prisonpolicy.org/reports/pie2017women.html, accessed July 23, 2018.

19. OpenInvest, "Who's in Prison in America," https://www.openinvest .co/blog/statistics-prison-america, accessed July 27, 2018.

20. Jennifer Gonnerman, "Before the Law," *New Yorker*, October 6, 2014, https://www.newyorker.com/magazine/2014/10/06/before-the-law.

21. Human Rights Watch, "Not in It for Justice," https://www.hrw.org/report/2017/04/11/not-it-justice/how-californias-pretrial-detention-and-bail-system-unfairly, accessed July 17, 2018.

22. David Riley, "Report: Rochester Tops 'Extreme Poverty' List," *Democrat & Chronicle* (Rochester, NY), January 8, 2015, https://www.democrat andchronicle.com/story/news/2015/01/08/rochester-poverty-act-community-foundation-report/21452093.

23. Emily Badger and Kevin Quealy, "How Effective Is Your School District? A New Measure Shows Where Students Learn the Most," *New York Times*, December 5, 2017, https://www.nytimes.com/interactive/2017/12/05/upshot/a-better-way-to-compare-public-schools.html?smid=fb-share.

24. hooks, *Teaching to Transgress*.

25. Ransby, *Ella Baker*.

26. John Britton, "Interview with Ella Baker: June 19, 1968," Civil Rights Oral History Project, Moorland-Spingarn Collection, Howard University.

27. Ransby, *Ella Baker*.

28. Ibid.

29. Ibid.

CHAPTER 4: GRIT, ZEST, AND RACISM (THE HUNGER GAMES)

1. Michael Watz, "An Historical Analysis of Character Education," *Journal of Inquiry and Action in Education* 4, no. 2 (2011): 3.

2. Ibid.

3. Elizabeth Levesque, "What Does Civics Education Look Like in America?," *Brookings*, July 23, 2018, https://www.brookings.edu/blog/brown-center-chalkboard/2018/07/23/what-does-civics-education-look-like-in-america.

4. Ibid.

5. Devon Black, "The Importance of Civics Education in Local Politics," *Harvard Political Review* (January 15, 2018), http://harvardpolitics.com/united-states/the-importance-of-civics-education-in-local-politics.

6. Meira L. Levinson, "The Civic Empowerment Gap: Defining the Problem and Locating Solutions," Digital Access to Scholarship at Harvard, 2010, https://dash.harvard.edu/bitstream/handle/1/8454069/Levinson%20 The%20Civic%20Empowerment%20Gap.pdf?sequence=1&isAllowed=y.

7. Carnegie Corporation of New York and CIRCLE, *The Civic Mission of Schools* (New York: Carnegie Corporation of New York, 2003).

8. Character LAB, "Character Strengths," https://www.characterlab.org.

9. Rene Stutzman and Bianca Prieto, "Trayvon Martin Shooting: Screams, Shots Heard on 911 Call," *Orlando Sentinel*, March 12, 2012,

http://www.orlandosentinel.com/news/seminole/os-trayvon-martin-shooting
-911-call-20120316-story.html.

10. Character LAB, "Character Strengths."

11. Ty Tagami, "New Georgia Analysis: See If Your School 'Beat the
Odds,'" *Atlanta Journal-Constitution*, December 21, 2017, https://www.ajc
.com/news/state--regional-education/georgia-releases-new-analysis-school
-performance/lDKeAaHqyvnmFZR22NUoPI.

12. Ibid.

13. Centers for Disease Control and Prevention, "Adverse Childhood
Experiences," https://www.cdc.gov/violenceprevention/acestudy/index.html,
accessed February 19, 2018.

14. American School Counselor Association, "State-By-State Student-
to-Counselor Ratio Report: 10 Year Trends," https://www.schoolcounselor
.org/asca/media/asca/home/Ratios14–15LowestToHighest.pdf, accessed
August 1, 2018.

15. Ibid.

16. Laura Pappano, "'Trauma-Sensitive Schools': A New Framework for
Reaching Troubled Students," *Harvard Education Letter* 30, no. 3 (May/June
2014), http://hepg.org/hel-home/issues/30_3/helarticle/trauma-sensitive
-schools.

17. Jeffrey A. Snyder, "Teaching Kids 'Grit' Is All the Rage. Here's
What's Wrong With It," *New Republic*, May 6, 2014, https://newrepublic
.com/article/117615/problem-grit-kipp-and-character-based-education.

18. Robert G. Lee, *Orientals: Asian Americans in Popular Culture* (Philadelphia: Temple University Press, 1999).

19. Ellen McGirt, "The Model Minority Myth," *Fortune*, April 17, 2017,
http://fortune.com/2017/04/17/the-model-minority-myth.

20. Kat Chow, "'Model Minority' Myth Again Used as a Racial Wedge
Between Asians and Blacks," *Code Switch*, National Public Radio, April 19,
2017, https://www.npr.org/sections/codeswitch/2017/04/19/524571669
/model-minority-myth-again-used-as-a-racial-wedge-between-asians-and
-BlacksChow.

21. Angela Duckworth, *Grit: The Power of Passion and Perseverance*
(New York: Scribner, 2016).

22. Ibid.

23. Ibid.

24. Natasha Bertrand, "Atlanta Is the Most Unequal City in America—
Here's Why," *Business Insider*, March 20, 2015, http://uk.businessinsider
.com/atlanta-is-the-most-unequal-city-in-america--heres-why-2015-3?IR=T.

25. David Leonhardt, "In Climbing Income Ladder, Location Matters,"
New York Times, July 22, 2013, https://www.nytimes.com/2013/07/22/business
/in-climbing-income-ladder-location-matters.html.

26. Bertrand, "Atlanta Is the Most Unequal City in America."

27. Max Blau, "Has Intown Atlanta Lost Affordable Housing for Good?," *Atlanta Magazine*, March 1, 2016, http://www.atlantamagazine.com /homeandgarden/has-intown-atlanta-lost-affordable-housing-for-good.

28. Annie E. Casey Foundation blog, "As Atlanta's Economy Thrives, Many Residents of Color Are Left Behind," June 24, 2015, http://www.aecf .org/blog/as-atlantas-economy-thrives-many-residents-of-color-are-left-behind.

29. Ty Tagami, "Atlanta's New 'Chronically Failing' Schools," *Atlanta Journal-Constitution*, January 17, 2017, https://www.ajc.com/news/local -education/atlanta-new-chronically-failing-schools/Jn3sGxJotobMnmx AwmK9ZJ.

30. Maurice J. Hobson, *The Legend of the Black Mecca: Politics and Class in the Making of Modern Atlanta* (Chapel Hill: University of North Carolina Press, 2017).

31. Morris, *Pushout*.

32. Deb Belt, "Atlanta Ranked No. 1 for Sex Trafficking; Conventions to Blame?" *Buckhead Path*, March 13, 2014, https://patch.com/georgia /buckhead/atlanta-ranked-no-1-for-sex-trafficking-conventions-to-blame.

33. Melinda D. Anderson, "Why the Myth of Meritocracy Hurts Kids of Color," *Atlantic*, July 27, 2017, https://www.theatlantic.com/education /archive/2017/07/internalizing-the-myth-of-meritocracy/535035.

34. Ibid.

CHAPTER 5: ABOLITIONIST TEACHING, FREEDOM DREAMING, AND BLACK JOY

1. Baldwin, *The Price of the Ticket*.

2. Claudia Rankine, *Citizen: An American Lyric* (Minneapolis: Graywolf Press, 2014).

3. Nick Wing, "Our Bail System Is Leaving Innocent People to Die in Jail Because They're Poor," *Huffington Post*, July, 14, 2016, https://www .huffingtonpost.com/entry/cash-bail-jail-deaths_us_57851f50e4b0e05f052381cb.

4. Ibid.

5. Angela Y. Davis, *Abolition Democracy: Beyond Empire, Prisons, and Torture* (New York: Seven Stories Press, 2005).

6. Harvard Square Library, "Garrison, Williams Lloyd (1805-1879)," http://www.harvardsquarelibrary.org/biographies/william-lloyd-garrison, accessed March 3, 2018.

7. Kendi, *Stamped from the Beginning*.

8. "For Stanton, All Women Were Not Created Equal," *All Things Considered*, National Public Radio, July 13, 2011, https://www.npr.org/2011/07/13 /137681070/for-stanton-all-women-were-not-created-equal.

9. Carol Faulkner, *Lucretia Mott's Heresy: Abolition and Women's Rights in Nineteenth-Century America* (Philadelphia: University of Pennsylvania Press, 2011).

10. Henry Box Brown, *Narrative of the Life of Henry Box Brown* (Oxford, UK: Oxford University Press, 2002), 60.

11. C. B. Dillard, "Learning to (Re)member the Things We've Learned to Forget," *Qualitative Inquiry and Global Crises* (2011): 226.

12. Tom Feelings, *The Middle Passage: White Ships/Black Cargo* (New York: Dial Books, 2018).

13. Robin D. G. Kelley, *Freedom Dreams: The Black Radical Imagination* (Boston: Beacon Press, 2002).

14. Kagiso Mnisi, "The Promise of Futurism Part 3: Content in the Digital Age, a Conversation with Lindokuhle Nkosi," *This Is Africa*, July 31, 2015, https://thisisafrica.me/%E2%80%A8the-promise-futurism-part-3 -content-digital-age-conversation-lindokuhle-nkosi.

15. Kelley, *Freedom Dreams*.

16. Ibid.

17. Maxine Greene, *Releasing the Imagination: Essays on Education, the Arts, and Social Change* (San Francisco: Jossey-Bass, 1995).

18. Clayborne Carson and Kris Shepard, eds., *A Call to Conscience: The Landmark Speeches of Dr. Martin Luther King, Jr.* (New York: Grand Central Publishing, 2001).

19. Joyce E. King, ed., *Black Education: A Transformative Research and Action Agenda for the New Century* (New York: Routledge, 2006).

20. Julie Depenbrock, "Federal Judge Finds Racism Behind Arizona Law Banning Ethnic Studies," *All Things Considered*, National Public Radio, August 22, 2017, https://www.npr.org/sections/ed/2017/08/22/ 545402866/federal-judge-finds-racism-behind-arizona-law-banning-ethnic -studies.

21. Darrin Hoop, "Why the Seattle Strike Matters," *Jacobin*, September 11, 2015, https://www.jacobinmag.com/2015/09/seattle-teachers-strike -standardized-testing-racial-justice.

22. Lydia O'Connor, "Many Seattle Parents Come Out in Support of Striking Teachers," *Huffington Post*, September 9, 2015, https://www .huffingtonpost.com/entry/seattle-teacher-strike-brings-out-concerned -parents_us_55f05a2be4b002d5c077859b.

23. Jesse Hagopian, "Standardized Testing Battle in Seattle: Union Votes for a Complete Moratorium on All Standardized Tests!," *I Am an Educator*, June 14, 2018, https://iamaneducator.com/2018/06/14/standardized -testing-battle-in-seattle-union-votes-for-a-complete-moratorium-on-all -standardized-tests.

24. Michael Hansen, "Which States Might Experience the Next Wave of Teacher Strikes?," *Brookings*, April 13, 2018, https://www.brookings.edu /blog/brown-center-chalkboard/2018/04/13/which-states-might-experience -the-next-wave-of-teacher-strikes.

25. United We Dream, "Our Mission," https://unitedwedream.org /heretostay, accessed April 2, 2018.

26. Taryn Finley, "This Kid's Letter to His Teacher for 'Lying' About Christopher Columbus Needs to Be Framed," *Huffington Post*, January 24, 2018, https://www.huffingtonpost.com/entry/journal-entry-lying-christopher -columbus_us_5a675a1fe4b0dc592a0cf121.

27. Lindsey Ellefson, "Parkland Survivors Rip Politician's 'Pathetic' Responses," CNN.com, February, 20, 2018, https://www.cnn.com/2018/02/19 /politics/parkland-survivors-cnntv/index.html.

28. Ibid.

29. Black Youth Project 100, "Agenda to Build Black Futures," http:// agendatobuildBlackfutures.org, accessed August 23, 2018.

30. Dream Defenders, "Freedom Papers," https://www.dreamdefenders .org, accessed June 17, 2018.

31. Prince George's County Board of Education, "Resolution Regarding Black Lives Matter at School," http://educationvotes.nea.org/wp-content /uploads/2018/02/Black-Lives-Matter-at-Schools-Week.pdf, accessed June 19, 2018.

32. DC Area Educators for Social Justice: A Project for Teaching Change, "Black Lives Matter Week of Action," https://www.dcareaeducators 4socialjustice.org/Black-lives-matter-week-faq, accessed June 17, 2018.

33. List compiled by Lynnette Mawhinney.

34. Justin Murphy, "'They're Like My Kids': RCSD Teacher Helps Transform Her Students with Nurturing Approach," *Democrat & Chronicle* (Rochester, NY), May 19, 2018, https://www.democratandchronicle.com /story/news/2018/05/19/rcsd-students-attendance-victorious-minds-academy -school-39-rochester-school-greenaway/547305002.

35. Ibid.

36. Astead W. Herndon, "This Former 'Teacher of the Year' Wants to Be Connecticut's First Black Democrat in Congress," *New York Times*, August 14, 2018, https://www.nytimes.com/2018/08/14/us/politics/jahana-hayes -teacher-connecticut.html.

37. Ewan Palmer, "Who Is Mandy Manning? Teacher of the Year Who Handed Trump Letters from Refugee Students During Silent Protest," *Newsweek*, May 3, 2018, https://www.newsweek.com/who-mandy-manning -teacher-year-who-handed-trump-letters-refugee-students-909114.

38. Robin D. G. Kelley, "Coates and West in Jackson," *Boston Review*, December 22, 2017, http://bostonreview.net/race/robin-d-g-kelley-coates-and -west-jackson.

39. Ibid.

40. Ibid.

41. Ibid.

42. Ann Helms, "Bree Newsome, James Tyson Talk About SC Confederate Flag Grab," *Charlotte Observer*, July 6, 2015, http://www.charlotte observer.com/news/local/article26578984.html.

43. Allies for Change, "Who We Are," http://www.alliesforchange.org /intro.html, accessed July 5, 2018.

44. Emily Chiariello, "Why Talk About Whiteness?," *Teaching Tolerance* (Summer 2016), https://www.tolerance.org/magazine/summer-2016/why-talk -about-Whiteness.

45. Ibid.

46. Brittney Cooper, *Eloquent Rage: A Black Feminist Discovers Her Superpower* (New York: St. Martin's Press, 2018), 275.

47. National Research Council, *Preparing Teachers: Building Evidence for Sound Policy* (Washington, DC: National Academies Press, 2010).

48. Audre Lorde, "Age, Race, Class, and Sex: Women Redefining Difference," Copeland Colloquium, Amherst College, April 1980, reprinted in *Sister Outsider: Essays and Speeches* (Freedom, CA: Crossing Press, 1984).

CHAPTER 6: THEORY OVER GIMMICKS

1. hooks, *Teaching to Transgress*.

2. Barry M. Goldenberg, "White Teachers in Urban Classrooms: Embracing Non-White Students' Cultural Capital for Better Teaching and Learning," *Urban Education* 49, no. 1 (2014): 111–44.

3. US Census Bureau, "State and County Quick Facts." Data derived from population estimates, American Community Survey, Census of Population and Housing, County Business Patterns, Economic Census, Survey of Business Owners, Building Permits, Census of Governments (2010).

4. Poppy Harlow and Hatley Draznin, "Mellody Hobson on Race: 'We Must Be Color Brave,'" CNN.com, January 22, 2018, http://money.cnn.com /2018/01/22/news/mellody-hobson-boss-files/index.html.

5. Jennifer Calfas, "Was Starbucks' Racial Bias Training Effective? Here's What These Employees Thought," *Time*, May 30, 2018, http://time .com/5294343/starbucks-employees-racial-bias-training.

6. Ibid.

7. Michael Eric Dyson, in foreword to Robin DiAngelo, *White Fragility: Why It's So Hard for White People to Talk About Racism* (Boston: Beacon Press, 2018), ix.

8. Leigh Patel, "Trump and Settler Colonialism," *CTheory* (December 1, 2017), http://ctheory.net/ctheory_wp/trump-and-settler-colonialism.

9. NYC Stands with Standing Rock, "#Standing Rock Syllabus," https:// nycstandswithstandingrock.wordpress.com/standingrocksyllabus, accessed June 19, 2018.

10. Scott Morgensen, "Standing Rock Solidarity Toolkit," *Standing Up for Social Justice*, http://nb.showingupforracialjustice.org/standing_rock _solidarity, accessed August 23, 2018.

11. Alleen Brown, "Five Spills, Six Months in Operation: Dakota Access Track Record Highlights Unavoidable Reality—Pipeline Leak," *Intercept*, January 9, 2018, https://theintercept.com/2018/01/09/dakota-access -pipeline-leak-energy-transfer-partners.

12. Morgensen, "Standing Rock Solidarity Toolkit."

13. Christine E. Sleeter, "Critical Race Theory and Education," in *Encyclopedia of Diversity in Education*, ed. James A. Banks (Thousand Oaks, CA: SAGE, 2012), 491–95.

14. María C. Ledesma and Dolores Calderón, "Critical Race Theory in Education: A Review of Past Literature and a Look to the Future," *Qualitative Inquiry* 21, no. 3 (2015): 206–22.

15. Ibid.

16. Ibid.

17. Victoria M. Massie, "White Women Benefit Most from Affirmative Action—and Are Among Its Fiercest Opponents," *Vox*, June 23, 2016, https://www.vox.com/2016/5/25/11682950/fisher-supreme-court-White-women-affirmative-action.

18. Ibid.

19. Subini Ancy Annamma, *The Pedagogy of Pathologization: Dis/abled Girls of Color in the School-Prison Nexus* (New York: Routledge, 2017).

20. Tara J. Yosso, "Whose Culture Has Capital? A Critical Race Theory Discussion of Community Cultural Wealth," *Race Ethnicity and Education* 8, no. 1 (2005): 69–91.

21. Angela Locks, "Summary of Yosso's Cultural Wealth Model," California State University Long Beach, http://web.csulb.edu/divisions/aa/personnel/fcpd/workshops/documents/Wrk1EditedYossoCulturalWealthSummary.pdf.

22. Patricia Hill Collins, *Black Feminist Thought: Knowledge, Consciousness, and the Politics of Empowerment* (New York: Routledge, 2002).

23. Yolanda Sangweni, "Amen! Beyoncé's Coachella Performance Was the Ultimate Celebration of HBCs and Black Women," *Essence*, April 15, 2018, https://www.essence.com/entertainment/beyonc%C3%A9-coachella-performance-2018.

24. Taylor, *How We Get Free*, 3.

25. Ibid., 4.

26. Lisa Duggan, "The New Homonormativity: The Sexual Politics of Neoliberalism," in *Materializing Democracy: Toward a Revitalized Cultural Politics*, ed. Russ Castronovo and Dana D. Nelson (Durham, NC: Duke University Press, 2002), 175–94.

27. Jasbir Puar, "In the Wake of It Gets Better," *Guardian*, November 16, 2010, https://www.theguardian.com/commentisfree/cifamerica/2010/nov/16/wake-it-gets-better-campaign.

28. Michael Johnson, "The It Gets Better Project: A Study in (and of) Whiteness—in LGBT Youth and Media Cultures," in *Queer Youth and Media Cultures*, ed. Christopher Pullen (London: Palgrave Macmillan, 2014), 279.

29. Ibid.

30. Cathy J. Cohen, "Punks, Bulldaggers, and Welfare Queens: The Radical Potential of Queer Politics?," *GLQ* 3 (1997): 437–65.

31. E. Patrick Johnson, "'Quare' Studies, or (Almost) Everything I Know About Queer Studies I Learned from My Grandmother," *Text and Performance Quarterly* 21, no. 1 (2001): 1–25.

32. Ibid.

33. Joyce E. King, "Dysconscious Racism: Ideology, Identity, and the Miseducation of Teachers," *Journal of Negro Education* 60, no. 2 (1991): 133–46.

34. Ibid.

35. Robin DiAngelo, "White Fragility," *International Journal of Critical Pedagogy* 3, no. 3 (2011).

36. Cheryl E. Matias, *Feeling White: Whiteness, Emotionality, and Education* (Rotterdam: SensePublishers, 2016).

37. Move to End Violence: Building Movement for Social Change, "Ally or Co-Conspirator? What It Means to Act #InSolidarity," https://www.movetoendviolence.org/blog/ally-co-conspirator-means-act-insolidarity, accessed July, 25, 2018.

38. Elizabeth Martinez and Arnoldo Garcia, "What Is Neoliberalism?" *CorpWatch*, January 1, 1997, https://corpwatch.org/article/what-neoliberalism.

39. Matthew Cunningham-Cook, "Chicago Teachers Push Back Against Neoliberal Education Reform," *Nation*, September 11, 2012, https://www.thenation.com/article/chicago-teachers-push-back-against-neoliberal-education-reform.

40. Chicago Teachers Union, "The Schools Chicago's Students Deserve," https://www.ctunet.com/blog/schools-chicagos-students-deserve-presents-comprehensive-plan-to-improve-student-academic-performance-and-strengthen-neighborhood-schools, accessed June 23, 2018.

41. Ibid.

42. Patricia Hill Collins, *Black Sexual Politics: African Americans, Gender, and the New Racism* (New York: Routledge, 2004).

43. James Baldwin, "If Black English Isn't a Language, Then Tell Me, What Is?," *New York Times*, July 29, 1979, https://archive.nytimes.com/www.nytimes.com/books/98/03/29/specials/baldwin-english.html?_r=1.

CHAPTER 7: WE GON' BE ALRIGHT, BUT THAT AIN'T ALRIGHT

1. Ralph Ellison, "The World and the Jug," 1963, in *The Cambridge Companion to Ralph Ellison*, ed. Ross Posnock (Cambridge, UK: Cambridge University Press, 2005), 31.

2. Linda Villarosa, "Why America's Black Mothers and Babies Are in a Life or Death Crisis," *New York Times*, April 11, 2018, https://www.nytimes.com/2018/04/11/magazine/Black-mothers-babies-death-maternal-mortality.html?mtrref=www.google.com&gwh=7C4E5845F2BB0E38C290C6D487979B54&gwt=pay.

3. Ibid.

4. Ibid.

5. Ibid.

6. Gillian B. White, "Escaping Poverty Requires Almost 20 Years with Nearly Nothing Going Wrong," *CityLab*, April 28, 2017, https://www.citylab.com/life/2017/04/escaping-poverty-requires-almost-20-years-with-nearly-nothing-going-wrong/524727.

7. Emanuella Grinberg and Sheena Jones, "Georgia Officer Who Said 'We Only Kill Black People' to Retire," CNN.com, September 1, 2017, https://www.cnn.com/2017/08/31/us/georgia-cobb-county-officer-racial-comment-trnd/index.html.

8. Toni Cade Bambara, *The Salt Eaters* (New York: Vintage, 1980).

9. Ibid.

10. Ibid.

11. Kevin Quashie, *The Sovereignty of Quiet: Beyond Resistance in Black Culture* (Brunswick, NJ: Rutgers University Press, 2012).

12. *Daughters of the Dust*, dir. Julie Dash, American Playhouse, 1991.

13. W. E. B. Du Bois, *The Souls of Black Folk* (Chicago: A. C. McClurg, 1903).

14. Bakari Kitwana, *The Hip-Hop Generation: Young Blacks and the Crisis in African American Culture* (New York: Basic Civitas Books, 2003), 23.

15. Pat Parker, *An Expanded Edition of Movement in Black* (Ann Arbor, MI: Firebrand Books, 1999).

16. Wendy Kohli, "Teaching in the Danger Zone: Democracy and Difference," in *Democratic Social Education: Social Studies for Social Change*, ed. David W. Hurst and E. Wayne Ross (New York: Falmer Press, 2000), 23–42.

17. W. E. B. Du Bois, "My Evolving Program for Negro Freedom," *Clinical Sociology Review* 8, no. 1 (1990): 5.

18. Kendi, *Stamped from the Beginning.*

19. Nikki Giovanni, *Black Feeling, Black Talk/Black Judgement* (Detroit: Broadside Press, 1970).

20. W. E. B. Du Bois, "A Negro Nation Within the Nation," *Current History and Forum* 42, no. 3 (1935): 265.

INDEX